Internal Monologue

"A poetic journey through love and life"

April O. Wakefield-Spikener

Cover Design by Ashlei Reign

ISBN: 0692916911
ISBN-13: 978-0692916919
Revised

DEDICATION

For My God Given Angels, My Parents:
Loretta Roberts-Bennett
and Bennie Wakefield, Jr. (4/30/55-12/18/2011)
Thank you for giving me life. I hope that I have become
a woman who makes both of you proud.

For Nana…
I understand now.

For My Babies,
Avantae and Damani:
Don't ever let anyone else
tell you who you are
or who you can become.
If you can see it, you can be it.
If you want it, it's yours!
I love you.

For Love,
I reach the most amazing levels
in life when I can feel your presence.
I will always be all about you.

CONTENTS

Internal Monologue

Breath of Life

I finally decided to
end the procrastination
End the years
of my lack of dedication
put an end
to the excuses
that take control of me
I've decided to let my dreams breathe.
For so long
they've been suffocating
as if the air
was over polluted
because if ever I shared them,
I'd give the diluted
version.
Partial dreams, partial truth.
feel free to re-word it.
I said it
but never did it.
I wanted it
but always hid it.
So I'm putting an end to the excuses
that got the best of me.
I decided
to let my dreams breathe.

About Love

For those who believe
this life is about loving…
You.
The raw
the real
the truth.
Said they were being authentic
and actually meant it.
The ones who are brave enough
to be real.
To communicate
how they feel
whether angry
or sad
joyful or bad.
Those people…
the ones who understand
life is about love.

My Mama and God

They didn't have an agreement.
He forced me on her
shocked her
locked her
down
with me.
But He Blessed her...
Abundantly.
Although I'd be difficult
He was capable
of miracles
so every time
I needed her
she had Him.
Without question.
He just kept on
Blessing.
He made sure
she had it
whatever I'd need
so that she wasn't lacking
what was needed to build
this version of me.
He made ways
out of none
He brightened days
with no sun
He gave her me
and gave me her.
I thank God for my mama.

Starting 5

Today's a new day
but I still feel a lil'
unappreciated
A lil' looked over
and underestimated.
Just a little neglected
and undervalued.
Maybe it would change
if I took some time
now to
re-evaluate
your position in my life
your position in my heart
maybe I should bench you
and let someone else
start.
Maybe they'll appreciate
the opportunity
they've been given.
Pay some attention
to the end
and the beginning.
Take advantage
of the good
and let the bad go.
Or maybe
it would be all for show.
But at least
maybe
I'd feel appreciated.

Worryin'

Worryin'.
Stressin'.
Worryin'.
Pressin'.
Worryin'.
Tryin'.
Worryin'.
Cryin'.
Worryin'.
About somethin'.
But
Worryin'
Ain't never changed nothin'.

Love Is

Love is a feeling
The truth, undenied
The reason many have smiled
smiles of happiness
and others have cried.
Love is an emotion.
One that could never
be imitated.
A gesture, a word, a helping hand
greatly appreciated.
Love is a beautiful blue sky
on a bright summer's day
or those arms so gently
wrapped around you
when rain has come your way.
Love is an emotion
a word, a hug, a kiss…
Indescribable,
and undefinable.
That's what love is.

You Are

You are my sunshine on a rainy day
my umbrella to shield the rain
You are the jokes that bring laughter
which causes happiness
to erase my pain.
You are my pencil to my notebook
or ink inside a pen
You are the shoulder that I lean on
You are there through thick and thin.
You are the strings that help me
tie my shoes
or the soap that keeps me clean.
You are like the air I breathe,
Very necessary.
If you know what I mean.
You are the fingers that help me write.
You are the eyes that allow me to see.
You are so much more
than I could say in words
You are everything to me.

Daddy Issues

I kicked.
I screamed.
I judged.
The first two...
Figuratively.
The second...
Literally.
I didn't believe he loved me.
I needed a daddy.
A father.
A protector.
A guide.
I needed someone to love
all of the broken things
I had inside...
Tell me it would be alright.
And he couldn't.
Maybe he didn't know how...
But I didn't know that.
I didn't care until
I couldn't get those days back.
I spent too much time
Judging
So I had none left to understand.
He was doing the best he could...
as a father.
And giving what he knew how...
As a man.

The Past.

Memories.
I remember.
Memories.
I remember.
An unforgotten past.
Happiness.
Sadness.
Please don't even ask.
A trying time.
A life changing experience.
an outcome so great.
Growth.
Development.
Who I am today.
Memories.
I remember.
Memories.
I remember.
Memories.
Always last.
But who would we be
In the present and future
Without memories of the past?

Butterfly

I was told if I love you
I should let you go
and if you really loved me
you'd come back and let me know.
Because when you're in love
nothing else feels right
so I decided to let you go
and you'd be my butterfly.
So if you fly around and
another flower catches your eye
Don't worry about what color it is
remember that love is blind.
Don't worry about the past
the present is all you need to see
and fate will lead you back
if we were meant to be.
I don't ever want you to sit and worry
and I never want you to cry
just know I let you go because I love you
and you're my butterfly.

TODAY

Blessed with another chance today.
Mistakes of yesterday are the past.
Today is my beginning.
Today I'll do new things
and do old things better.
Offer a smile to someone
without one
or maybe just enjoy the weather.
Maybe I'll lend a helping hand
to someone in desperate need
or offer faith to someone
who still does not believe.
Today I'll do new things.
Today is my beginning.
Because today I'm Blessed
With another chance.

Reflection

Looking back on the past.
School, friends, relationships,
all that didn't last.
The tears, the heartbreaks,
the love that wasn't love.
The reason change was needed
and so often thought of.
Looking back
on all that wasn't
and could never be
Everyone who once
meant so much to me.
Everything I wanted
to hold onto
But my hands couldn't grasp.
The good times
that I prayed would last.
Awesome times,
Awesome friends,
even the funniest of the funny jokes.
The poems that the tears
and the smiles wrote.
The song that constantly
plays in my heart,
The chosen selection.
I am thankful for the years
that inspired this reflection.

No Better

Hear the comments rolling off my tongue
the negativity escaping through my lips
I wonder if his eyes are on the prize
examining the movement of her hips.
And I speak whatever enters my mind
thinking he somehow agrees
and my words go in his right ear and out his left
imagining how she can fulfill his needs.
I ramble on about how her man doesn't care
"He has so many friends on the side"
and I constantly say "Well, she should've known."
when tears start to fall from her eyes.
I offer her no sympathy
she should've been aware of his dog status
from the start
and it was just bound to happen
he was bound to break her heart.
But who am I to speak upon
what is completely invisible to me?
Who I am to pretend my eyes
would have seen what hers didn't see?
Who am I to comment on her love
and where would I find the nerve?
Who the hell told me my relationship
was any better than hers?

Always Missing You

For so long I've tried to convince myself
that you'll eventually just be a part of my past
but the more I try to push your memory away
the longer it seems to last.
I even try to give others a chance
hoping maybe they'll fill the space
but every time
I end up back where I started
because no one can take your place.
Sometimes I just want to give up
because it seems there's no hope for us at all
but even when I just want to establish a friendship
my pride just won't let me call.
Over and over again I tell myself
there's just no explanation for love
But in the end,
when the others are gone
You're all that I'm thinking of.
Every time love comes to an end
I always find one cause to be true
That no matter who plays a role in my life,
it seems that I'm always missing you.

The Struggle

Month to month
Week to week
Check to check
How are you livin'?
Comfortable?
Or lackin' respect?
For yourself?
Are you hustlin' for a dollar?
Or selling yourself for a dime?
Are you the problem
instead of the solution?
Are you the cause of the crime?
The lie?
The need for the hustle?
How are you standing strong
in the struggle?

Straight Through My Heart

I thought I'd find everlasting love
and once it was perfect
we'd never be a part.
I thought I'd hold on to what was good
but it passed straight through my heart.
It's hard to hold on to
or even get a tight grip
on what's so perfect for you.
It's even harder when you give your all
putting your pride on the line
but all you do is fall.
Makes no sense
when love drives your heart insane
and the one you love
makes you feel so ashamed.
I thought true love lasts forever
for sure we wouldn't be apart
But a love so true
couldn't be held onto
and it passed straight through my heart.

The Day He Left Me For Her

He told me he was sorry
and that he loved me
He said he would do right by me
if we ever gave us another try.
But he said she would've told me
if he didn't.
That's the only reason he gave me for why.
It wasn't good enough
I needed more answers
What was I supposed to do
the day he left me for her?
Everyone said he was a fool
said they wouldn't have made that mistake
But they didn't even know
the right words to say
when they noticed my heart
start to break.
It felt like the end of the world
no shoulders to lean on
nowhere to turn
I was living in a world all by myself
the day he left me for her.

Remembering You

I remember when it was you and me
sneaking around just to be alone.
Finding the most private place to kiss
even calling each other on the phone.
I remember the smiles brought
from all of the love
and finally realizing it was true.
I remember how good you made me feel…
I remember losing you.
I remember trying so hard to get you
writing and calling to make my words clear
even telling myself to leave you alone
knowing I still wanted you here.
I remember just the other night
when I had you close enough to feel
I had you right there in my arms
and the whole moment was so real.
I remember when I brought myself
to realize
I still care and my feelings are true.
It feels good to be remembering love.
It feels good to be remembering you.

What We Call Friendship

Tell me what a friend is
or tell me what they're like.
Tell me they bring good and bad
or tell me I'm not right.
Is a friend someone who's close with all your enemies
and always in your face?
Is it someone who's attracted to your man?
Someone who'd do anything to take your place?
Is a friend someone who takes advantage of you
and sets you up to fall?
Is it someone who steers you in the wrong direction
and then isn't there for you at all?
Is a friend someone who calls you their friend
but feels the friendship has no worth?
Is it someone who spends time with your man
and then says "I'm sorry, but he came at me first?"
Is a friend someone who talks behind your back
or always changes your words to something else?
Is it someone who'd feel lots of pleasure
to see you by yourself?
Is a friend someone who's never on your side
and they hate you for whatever you do?
Is it someone who sees all your good as bad?
Someone who has never been down for you?
If this is what we call friendship
then it can only get worse in the end
and I guess the fact of the matter is
It's better to have a true enemy
than a true friend.

Never Explain

People always wonder
why I refuse to give my all
or why there are feelings
in the beginning
and then I never write or call.
They wonder what's the problem
what did they do
or what's holding me back
they wonder if I'm ever sincere
or if the relationship is all an act.
But once they find out the reason
it's just too hard for them to understand
why I'm still willing to give my all
to someone who has never been my man.
They can never understand the feelings
that have only been given to you
or why I try to care for them
when my feelings for you are so true.
I can barely understand it myself
but this love drives my heart insane
and that fact that I want it back
is one I can never explain.

For Those

For those who came before me
slaving everyday out in the field
singing, praying, hoping, dreaming
a day like this would be real.
For those who sat in the back of
the bus
and only drank water
from the colored section….
To them I owe this poetry selection.
For those who never believed
Black is beautiful
or thought women should stand
in the back and never speak.
The ones who never understood
that beauty is only skin deep.
For those who didn't think
women should vote
or have rights equal
to those of a man.
This is for those who actually
believed
they could control God's plan.
For those who don't understand
love is blind
and your heart is more important
than the color of your skin
The ones who let the appearance
of flesh
be the deciding factor
instead of the knowledge that lies
within.
This is for those who thought
I'd never succeed in school
because they didn't think
I had what it took
and for those who thought negative
of me
because they judged me
based on my looks.
This is for those who held me up
when I couldn't stand on my own
two feet.
These two words are for those
who always
or never
believed in me:
Thank You.

Write You Away

Your memory
is a burden on my mind
A never ending pain in my heart.
A "Wish I would have
made the right decision"
kind of situation
Perfection that never got its start.
A joy that was never held onto.
A true happiness
taken away too fast.
A love that was sewn into my heart;
But still a love that didn't last.
Your memory is one to which
I have many feelings
but still can't find the words to say
I wish it was one I couldn't remember
I wish I could write you away.

We Were

We used to be sisters.
The inseparable kind.
Anytime you thought of me
she would also come to mind.
Closer than two best friends
we shared so many good laughs
she was the best friend
I never admitted to have
because we used to be sisters.
We were those kind of sisters
where you had to respect both of us
because if you didn't
the other would make a fuss.
Joined together at the hip
until one day
there was a drastic change.
And when asked
"Is that your family?"
she replied,
"We used to be."

Private

I'm a very private person
but I'm deeper than the depth of any sea.
I'm brighter than the sun
on its brightest day
there's so much more than
what meets the eye with me.
I'm a very private person.
As private as solitary confinement
or limo tint on a limousine.
Extremely private.
If you know what I mean.
I'm not gonna broadcast my business
or play my life story out loud
I'm not gonna yell over you
just to be noticed in a crowd
and I'm not gonna get wild.
I won't do things
to make myself look stupid
just to get some extra attention
that's just not me.
Because just like I mentioned…
I'm a very private person.
I'm deeper than the depth of the sea
I'm brighter than the sun on its brightest day
There's so much more than what meets the eye with me.

By My Side

It's love and I know it
because I feel it wherever you touch
I just haven't found the right time
to tell you I love you so much.
The butterflies in my stomach
have their own little town
because every time you're near
they start flying around.
I know the love is true
because it's too strong for me to hide
and I know I'll be okay
as long as you are by my side.
I feel you with every heartbeat
I breathe you with every breath I take
I see your face every time I blink
and miss you seconds after you go away.
It's love and I know it
and it's so much stronger than pride
and I know I'll be okay
as long as you are by my side.

Past in the Past

It took so long but now I know
you can't make someone care
more than they do
and I realize you can love who you want
but can't make them only love you.
Thinking back to the time
when he was so perfect
but once I let go I couldn't grab back on
and there was no way
to take back yesterday
when he began to love someone.
And I think back to the time
when he was all I knew
and I never questioned what our love
was worth
I never pictured me by myself
until the day he left me for her.
Sometimes it's really hard to let go
and you try to hide feelings
that continue to last
but everything that happens
happens for a reason
so it's best to keep the past in the past.

Make Things Better

It's strange how you can't see clear
until the chance is no longer yours
and then how you finally realize what you had
but you can't get back through that door.
So you sit and wonder what do you do
when the past has passed you by
and all of a sudden your heart lets in
a feeling it once denied.
The good things you did once before
no longer mean the same
and the love that you now wish was yours
is filed under someone else's name.
How can you bring the past to the future
when you realize you've made a mistake
and where do you find the tools to mend
a heart you didn't mean to break?
No one has the right answer to give
so how do you piece it back together?
You must find the world's only instructions
on "How to Make Things Better."

Miles In Between

No matter how much time goes by
nothing changes the way I feel
and when I say to you "I love you"
I can't find any other feeling as real.
And even though you don't let me grab on
to the one thing I would keep
I think of you every hour I'm awake
sometimes I even dream of you when I sleep.
For you I have this burning flame
that may never even begin to go out
because the feelings that I have for you
are the only feelings I do not doubt.
If we ever get the chance our love deserves
nothing will tear us apart
because true love can't fade
It's kept within our hearts.
You create my happiest moments
your love is the greatest sight I've ever seen
and nothing can change the way I feel
not even the miles in between.

Never

I had never felt this way before.
No never.
I never thought I'd pray for more.
Not ever.
But I was wrong.
I found myself stuck in a feeling so strong
where I'd hurt so bad and have to ask why
and I'd find myself creating such a lie.
All the things I said I'd never do
I made exceptions for
when I found you.
But the pain in my heart
would last so long
convincing myself
that you just weren't wrong.
The things I said I'd never forgive you for
are things I'd take back
because that was poor.
I said I wouldn't forgive you for not loving me
but I would
I'd give your heart time
because I know you could.
Even if we're not
or won't ever be together
My heart wouldn't be free
if I made never last forever.

I Miss Oakland

I miss Oakland.
My people.
The culture.
The realness.
I think I ran away
One day.
Never looking back.
Never wanted to.
Wanted to escape
the disappointment
the heartbreak
the death.
Felt like there was nothing
left.
And then one day my heart remembered...
This
is home.

Sacrifice

We're all put here for a reason
our names and futures are already planned
But once we leave and go back home
our loved ones don't understand.
When we die young everyone believes
that we had so much in store
but they fail to realize we did what was planned
God felt the world didn't need us anymore.
Isn't is strange how tomorrow is never promised
and people die in such pain?
Still we cry because they're gone
and all sunshine turns to rain.
What if the life He granted them
was meant to be short lived
and the time they gave to others
was all they were here to give.
What if my life was created to save you
so that you won't bow your head with pity and sorrow
and since I'm here to make your life better
I won't wake up tomorrow.
Only when there are lessons learned
do we do what we feel is right
So what if for us to be successful
someone else had to be sacrificed?

Seems Like Too Much

If saying "I care about you" seems like too much,
Don't say it.
If saying "I miss you" is too much
Don't say it.
If saying "I need you" seems like too much
Don't say it.
If saying "I love you" seems like too much
Don't say it.
Just wait.
Wait until you've exhausted your chance and it's too late.
Wait until I'm gone
when things that were once too much
are now not enough.
Wait until your heart
can't help but to feel what it feels
but it only matters to you.
So don't say a thing,
if saying how you feel
seems like too much.

Know You

When I look at you
I can only assume
but when I assume I'm so far off.
I think that your life has no worries
I think that you will pay no cost.
In your eyes I see a twinkle
that I can't ever see in my own
and it appears that you're so happy
even though you're all alone.
I see you creating your own sunshine
you brighten your own day
so there's no rain
and when you get a taste of hurt
you protect yourself from the pain.
It appears you have so much strength
and that is the reason you smile
it seems like the happy times in your life
go on for miles and miles.
But once I speak to you things change
your life is no better than mine
and that twinkle that I saw
was just a tear forming in your eye.
The strength that I saw in you
was nothing but a disguise
a way to keep yourself busy
so you don't think of all the lies.
But now that we've spoken
I finally see the truth
and I see how much of your rain
looked like sunshine
all because I didn't know you.

All The Times

No matter how much was given
or accepted between us
it seems that what we shared
wasn't love or lust.
The effort you made
was the most I'd ever seen
yet I couldn't understand why
you wanted me as your queen.
Your heartbeat was so loud
I knew it beat for me
but the person that you dreamed of
was the one I couldn't be.
The smallest things you did
put a smile on my face
but even with you in my arms
there was still an empty space.
Still you gave and gave
hoping I would come around
but it seemed the more you tried
the more I let you down.
And still with all the times
you shared feelings so true
it seems that I
just couldn't love you.

Not Sorry

I'm sorry if you are offended.
I realize you may be wondering
why it ended
or who it ended
with.
I realize you have relationship and friendship
#goals
to uphold.
And my life may be confusing
with the truth told.
The thing is
you just never know
If it's your truth
or mine
that has the world blind...
That fills these lines
on these pages.
The truth is just that
regardless of our ages
and I said I'm sorry
but I'm actually not.
It is what it is.

After The Rain

I've cried more tears
than the average person
but all you see is the sunshine.
The light.
You don't realize
I've been broken...
So much that
I'm wide open.
So it's really the hurt,
the tears,
the appreciation
that all the years
of pain
are turning around.
Sunshine
from the clouds.
It's gratefulness.

Layoff

Trying to be politically correct
with my feelings
but the reality of the situation
will cause some of us
to need healing.
My heart is on the ground
in a million pieces
searching for the
five million reasons
I'm being laid off.
No pay off.
Just let go.
Just a thank you
for your time
and a letter
with a logo.
Just a politically correct
lay off notice
Just a professional way
of saying good-bye.
Just an official reality notice
saying what I worked
so hard for
faded away with time.
Just a firm
hand shake
and a very sincere smile
with an official good-bye…
for now.

Transition

I've never been in a place
like this.
Heartbroken.
Confused.
Angry.
Sad.
Don't know how to accept
the fact
that what I had
is gone.
No longer mine
but still not belonging
to anyone else.
So I'm stuck.
Heartbroken.
Confused.
Angry.
Sad.
In transition.

Paper

This is the sheet of paper
where I took down
her phone number and her name.
This is the paper that told me
you were to blame.
This is the paper
that brought out your lies.
This is the paper
that caught the tears
falling from my eyes.
This is the paper
that showed me
what I felt before
Evidence says:
You don't really love me
anymore.

Life

Life is what you make it
nothing more, nothing less
you have to learn your lesson
after you get the test.
No tears and
no whining
will help you to get by
Strength and determination
will help you survive.
Life is short
But you live it.
Through good times and through bad
through struggles and hard times
you'll breakdown
then you'll laugh.
Life gives only
one chance
Just one chance
to do your best.
Life is what you make it
nothing more, nothing less.

Brown Girl

I know we all love
love to love
want to love
the brown girl
But does the brown girl
love herself?
Soft caramel, dark chocolate,
even pecan or French vanilla
colored skin
strong, determined, eager
but so doubtful within.
Hard-core, soft heart,
loud mouth, soft spoken,
Brown pride, Black power
sometimes even the company's token
Girl.
Brown girl so hurt,
so angry about slavery's past
So determined to let
the world know
she'll get through
and make it last.
So fearful that her brown skin,
her Black skin
her African-American
could hold her back
needing to think about
all she possesses
and not the little she lacks.
I know we all love
love to love
want to love
need to love
the brown girl
but does the brown girl love herself?
Or does she seek validation
from someone else?

Pretty

People always told me
I was pretty.
I never believed them.
I couldn't see it.
I was always teased
as a kid...
Big forehead
thick eyebrows
hairy arms
all of it.
The boys I liked..
Crushes on my sister.
Even my "friends"
chose to kick it with her.
I was jealous.
So even when people told me
I was "pretty"
I didn't believe them.
I couldn't see it.
So there's no way
I could be it.
Took me over 20 years
to agree.
And now,
I don't need anyone
to validate me.
I'm so much more
than "pretty."

VIBE.

What's up baby, I'm Vibe.
I can run through your body
and your mind.
I'll bring out feelings
you didn't know were there
and cause problems in your life
even you can't bear.
I'll let you feel things
you never knew you could
and cause you to do things
just because they feel good.
I don't play games with you
I just bring out what hides
even if you believe
that all you feel is a lie.
Baby, I'm Vibe
and I am the truth.
That's why they send me
all through you.

Time.

Time has changed so many things
still I can't manage to change time.
Can't slow it down,
can't make it rewind.
Time is the cause for many things
so many things will never be the same.
Time has done so many things
because time has to change.

Special Friends

When I think of you
I think of what didn't happen
instead of remembering what did.
It seems that all of the let downs
somehow caused me to forget.
I remember a time you made me smile
so hard my jaws were sore
but I remember a time you made me cry
I didn't smile anymore.
Then there was a time you gave me hope
when all my hope was gone
you brought sunshine to my life
and then you moved on.
But still I loved you anyway
when you'd come and when you'd go
and I'd be satisfied having loved you
if it was all the love I'd know.
You showed me that miracles happen
even though you didn't try
and you taught me a lesson on life
when you'd leave or when you'd lie.
But now I cry before I smile
because I'm beginning to understand
that I'll love you
but I'll let you go
That's why we were special friends.

Never Doubt

Whether you're here or you're gone
I feel exactly the same
no jealousy or hurt
when someone mentions your name.
Insecurity walked away
when trust came back home
so now everything is secure
whether you're here
or you're gone.
It doesn't matter who you're talking to
or who you're standing by.
It doesn't matter
who's after you
there are no doubts
that you're mine.
When you hold me
there's love.
When you speak
it's all sincere.
Your hand somehow always there
to wipe the falling tears.
Whether you're with me or your friends
whether we're in or we're out
the love that you give
is the love I never doubt.

Live For You

Tomorrow's just another day
but what is guaranteed?
Who'll definitely be there for you
in your time of need?
Whose fingers wipe tears
from your eyes
each and every time you cry?
Whose love have you never doubted
and felt so deep inside?
Your own.
So live for you.
Regardless of who loves you today
the only love that's forever
is your own.
You're the only one
who always has your back
when everyone else is gone.
You're the only one
who controls your smile
even when skies are blue
So don't live life for everyone else
live your life for you!

Now Later

So many people are dying
so many lives coming to an end
It's evident that tomorrow is never promised
but not evident
that I love my family and friends.
In the midst of the tragedy
I began to cry
because it could've been your life
that ended that day
and I didn't even get to say goodbye.
I didn't tell you I love you
because I couldn't find the time
I didn't even pick up the phone
to call you
last week when you were on my mind.
I didn't bother to give you a hug
and tell you to "be safe" as you drove away.
I didn't tell you
how much you meant to me then
so I decided to tell you today.
It could've been you
whose life ended on such short notice
It could have been you
I cried for that day
so I'm telling you now
instead of later
three words I should never hesitate to say:
I Love You.

Picture

When I look at you
I see happiness, memories,
and sometimes pain.
You make me want to stop the present
and go back to you again.
It seems there's something special
when I have you in my hands
but you're just so small
sometimes your importance is hard
to understand.
You capture hearts
and leave holes and gaps
when you're gone
sometimes even making it hard
for some to go on.
But you're ever so great
capturing each moment in time
you make some days brighter
putting thoughts into my mind.
It seems you're so fragile
money can't even buy
what you're worth
holding so many special moments inside
yet you're only a picture.

Stranger to Love

Out the window
the trees blow
as Brian McKnight plays
I remember what I had
and who I was
but I'm such a stranger to love
these days.
Leaves fall like
ancient teardrops
reminding me of how
I yearn to once again
be who I was
but there's no changing
yesterday today
I'm such a stranger to love.

If Tomorrow Never Comes

Live today as the end
for you never know what's in store
tell your loved ones how you feel
before the chance is no longer yours.
Don't take for granted what's good for you
and always give your love
for what's done today
could be your last memory
if tomorrow never comes.
Don't put aside
what could be done today
and live your days to the fullest
because if you let life walk away
it will be the one thing
that you'll miss.
Think of others
when you go for yours
try to keep everyone on your side
for some of your friends
may not be your friends
and your enemies might keep you alive.
Don't take for granted what's good for you
and always give your love
for what's done today
could be your last memory
if tomorrow never comes.

Lonely Alone

It's like a tree with no leaves
or a pen with no ink
it's a sky with no sun
It's me alone and lonely.
I'm like a car without gas
or a camera with no film
I can't function correctly
when I know what's real.
I'm like hangers
with no clothes
or a newborn left on its own
It's me without love
feeling lonely alone.

Dorm Life

Dining Commons
or Student Union food
No choices, bad taste
nothing good enough to choose.
High rent, small rooms
bathrooms a disgust
bad hygiene, no home training
change is definitely a must.
And the people
are so different
personality and attitude wise
and the drama…
way too much
when it comes to dorm life.
Boys that should be men by now
females stuck in the past
time for a reality check
the reason why…
no need to ask.
High school mentality
attitude adjustments needed
rumors and lies
got all my homies heated.
Last year going through this
stressing day and night
everyone having problems
living this dorm life.

Just Like You

There's no doubt a difference between us:
The color of our skin is always seen.
But our insides hold the true meaning of us,
everything else falls somewhere in between.
Have you noticed the blood I shed is red
and the tears I cry are clear just as yours?
Still the struggles I have just go unsaid
running into closed doors, worse than before.
But I love people just the same as you
and I'm here for the same reasons you are.
Still what's false for you is for me what's true
the past puts you ahead of me by far.
The color does not determine the truth:
I bleed red, cry tears, and love.
Just like you.

Gratitude

Sometimes the only thing left to say
is thank you.
For the heartbreak
for the knife in my back
for the shade...
For the tears
for the hurt
for the bad days.
It's only through the pain
that we grow
that we come to know
who we are.
The real version.
It's the way we discover
that we are worth it.
The effort.
The sacrifice.
The long nights.
And sometimes
discovering that
takes a painful goodbye
or a forgiving hello.

Should Never

We should never be able
to fall in love
with people we can't have
or people who can't love us
back on the same level.
We shouldn't be allowed
to feel the pain
that heartbreak causes.
The feeling of taking losses
should be banned from our lives.
We should never have to cry
over loving someone
too much
or giving someone
the most precious parts
of us.
The memories
should never hurt.
Never make us question
our worth
because of them.
Love should never be a question
or a fear
or something we aren't allowed
to hold on to
when it's true.

Wrong Ones

I spent half of my lifetime
wishing people would love me
the way I needed to be
loved.
You know...
The people who are just as excited
about your birthday plans
as you are.
The ones who stay down
near or far.
The ones who celebrate your wins
and cry when you're sad…
Those kind of people
are a treasure to have
and to hold.
And I wanted people like those.
But I learned to love myself
because no one was consistent
or excited
or maybe I invited
the wrong ones
into my heart.

April Esquire

They told me I should be
an attorney
so many times
that my mind
believed it.
Thought it would be the best
option.
They said I liked to argue
so I would be great
I mean...
I was kind of good at debate...
So I believed it.
I wish they would have told me
to just dream.
That those "things"
I wanted to do
could be achieved.
That I could become anything
my heart desired.
I was inspired.
To write...
To sing...
But becoming an attorney
became "my dream"
until it wasn't.
When I discovered
I would be unhappy.
Rarely laughing
library studying
constantly covering...
someone else.
That wasn't what I wanted
for myself.
It was what they wanted
for me.
They should have told me
"Just dream baby."
"Just be… Amazing!"

The Family

I learned how to be broken
from the family.
How to not be open...
from the family.
I was "anti-social"
and "way too vocal"
and vulnerable
according to the family.
I learned how to keep secrets
from the family.
Learned to take what didn't belong
to me
from the family.
I became their victim...
The family's system
caused damage to me.
I learned how to not love me
from the family.
Originality wasn't a positive thing
in the family.
So I had no self-esteem
no building up of me...
From the family.
So many backwards role models
in the family
But I loved them past
the damaged me...
That was the "understanding" me.
But my mind was protected
because I was disrespected
so I couldn't respect it...
The family.

Ruined Me

He ruined me.
Showed me a love
no one else could make me feel
on more than one occasion.
He ruined me.
Told me he loved me
and this time it was for real
regardless of the "situation."
He ruined me.
Called me every morning
to make my morning good…
He ruined me.
Told me he adored me
and would always be there
if he could.
He ruined me.
Daily texts
daily calls
repeated I love yous
But still all
just to ruin me.

Blind

Every time I see her
post or text about her man
how they "made it"
through trials and tribulations...
I shake my head at the situation.
I just want to comment:
"Do you, Boo."
I know for a fact
her man ain't true.
I still remember
yesterday he asked where
I was at.
Matter of fact...
I still need to give him his hat back...
from the last time
he met up with a good friend of mine.
They say love makes you blind...
I'm starting to believe it.

The Realest

I could close my eyes
and plug my ears
and I'd still know
It's him when he touches me.
His energy...
My soul recognizes it
My body analyzes it...
Accepts it.
Respects it.
Connects.
With it.
It's the realest shit.
Ever.

Re-Routed

He was full of shit!
Fluent in my language.
The one that immediately
touches my heart
and calms my soul.
His voice made me feel
like I could conquer
any goal.
He made me feel whole.
But he was full of empty promises
Plenty of talk
no actions
lies were stacking
everything was lacking.
But my hopes were all the way up
by the time
I realized I shouldn't hope at all.
He took me high
and let me fall
onto everything
he couldn't deliver.

1. 8. 7.

Somebody killed my daddy.
Set a fire.
Let him burn.
Walked away.
Undetected.
Still I suspected...
Something wasn't right.
They said it was "likely"
An accident...
No cause determined...
No accelerant...
Located.
But the manner in which
he was located...
I was devastated.
He died.
Burned.
Today never again turned
into tomorrow.
For him.
And my soul still isn't
at peace
because my heart still believes
someone did it.
Purposely.
Decided my daddy
could go to heaven
almost a week
before Christmas.
That it was okay for him to miss this
important time
when he'd
finally meet my son.

Late Forgiveness

I was finally able to forgive
Myself.
For messing up
the most perfect love my heart ever felt.
Years later.
But for those years that passed...
I repeatedly asked
Myself
Why...
Why were you too afraid?
To jump in?
To take the chance?
To act now and understand
Later.
My soul loved him.
But my mind was too afraid
too guarded
too damaged
to believe
I could trust the feeling.
Didn't know that real love
provided healing.
Until it was too late.

Operation: Hustle

I knew so many hustlers.
Not because I was one
but I used to watch them
closely.
For long periods of time
mostly.
My mama wouldn't let me
go outside
when she wasn't home
and my sisters
weren't friendly
so I was alone
with my imagination
and the hustlers outside
with their situations.
They showed dedication...
and so many smooth
operations.
I'd love to give you the details
but it would be unfair
to put them on paper
they might still be out there...
hustlin'.

Heartbreak History

I remember all of the heartbreaks.
Forgot the feeling of the pain
but the stories...
I remember.
The first one...
He left me for someone else;
I wasn't ready.
The second one...
He left me for someone else;
She was "sexy."
The third one...
Fear and miscommunication;
High School heartbreak situation.
I hella loved him though.
Didn't really want to let him go.
There are some other shorter stories too...
Some temporary situations
some short term "Boos"
of no importance. No offense.
Oh yeah,
there was that one...
He wasn't over his Ex
I found out on the low
so I moved on to the next
with no hesitation.
Then there were some inbox situations...
No physical altercations.
No one is worth it.
I didn't deserve it...
The heartbreak.
But I'm thankful
for this extra page
of memories.

Searching for Broken

I don't think anyone
knows the real me...
Completely.
I opened up once.
Life lesson learned.
Trust and truth
must both be earned.
I'm waiting to find a friend
who's been so broken
that there's no judgement
when my heart opens
and my truth is spoken.
The broken ones understand the most
and judge the least.
They shine the brightest
and show up when you need
them.
I'm waiting for someone
completely imperfect
so I can share my truth
and leave the communication open.
I used to want to be perfect
but even I don't trust "perfect" people.

FREIGHT TRAIN

Everything
I ever wanted to feel
when it came to love
I felt
when I was next to him.
Everything.
But he came and he went.
Passing through my life
like an awakening.
Dropped off my magic
and kept it moving.
It was as if the train he was on
never stopped.
Just passed through
and slowed down long enough
for him to change my thoughts
Change my life...
Change me.
Magically.
He left me broken.
Open.
Just enough for the pain
to breathe
and the light to escape.
The pain hidden
by the smile on my face.
His love was real...
So it did the trick.
Left me feeling like... Magic.

Wednesday

I remember the Wednesday
I asked him for closure.
His behavior indicated
it was over
So I needed the words.
I approached.
Looked up at his face...
That was all she wrote.
He didn't give any...
Answers.
Looked...
Bothered.
Responded that now
wasn't the time.
No time was ever the time
because he was fine.
His face told me
I was blind.
The love was all in my mind.
I hated the look
in his eyes.
The way his head turned
to move on
that man I loved...
He was long gone.
And it was only Wednesday.

Hopeless Romantic

I'm that girl
that will watch the same
love story
play out over and over
again.
Fully engaged
until the very end.
I'm her.
That girl that can love
the same man
for eternity...
As long as it's real
between him and me.
HIM and ME.
As incorrect as that may be...
Grammatically.
I'm her.
I protect the memories.
The love.
The laughter.
Forever.
Because I'm the forever...
Always down for love
type.
I will always be her.

Skeletons

I don't have closets
for skeletons.
I set them free.
Give them air
let them breathe.
There's always an ear
willing to listen.
Someone who appreciates
my existence
enough to protect my words.
Even if their mind is temporarily
disturbed.
They forget what they've heard.
I just can't allow secrets
to eat me alive
to tear me up
and burn me inside...
I have to give them life.
Set them free
so the pain they cause
doesn't have an affect on me.
My skeletons...
They roam free
until they no longer exist.
There's no cemetery here.
and definitely no closet
full of skeletons.

All or Nothing

It was like he took me
to the cliff.
Together...
We agreed to jump.
Only he had a parachute
that I couldn't see
I was willing to risk it all
give him every ounce
of me
so together we would be free...
to love.
He needed security though.
So our life choice of jumping
in love together
was a one sided show
where love could not grow
because he was afraid
of the sacrifice.
Instead of deciding on happy
he chose safety.
The sadness of life without me
because she couldn't replace me.
But me...
I was willing to risk it all
jump without the parachute
and completely commit
to the fall
into my truth.
It was him I loved.

Broken Things

Sometimes
you let people in
and they break things.
Your valuables
Your antiques
Your trust...
Your heart.
Sometimes
they break things
that were supposed to be
off limits
from the start.
And then they part.
Walk away.
Disappear.
Blur your vision
to the point nothing is clear...
Anymore.
So be careful...
Yellow tape
Display box
Alarm system
whatever you need.
Use it wisely
so you don't have to deal
with more broken
"Things."

No Evidence.

I can't prove
he ever existed.
My heart has an imprint
of a true love being there
but I can't prove it.
I feel the emptiness
of what used to be
but I can't see his face.
I just know there's a space
that's empty.
Someone who touched my heart
and then left me.
I know what his love felt like
but I can't prove
he was ever real
I can't even prove
this is how I really feel.

Oh Well

I think of all the people
Who looked at me crazy
when I mentioned you
And our situation.
Maybe they caught
the revelation
that I missed.
Maybe they
heard it.
The stop sign that I ran
trying to get to
"My man"
How could they understand?
But it was me
who was blind
I should have opened my eyes
Tested the water
before jumping in...
Let you earn your place
as my friend.
I should have done that...
back then.
Too late now.

Move On

Today.
You stop.
Stop dreaming.
Stop believing.
Stop hoping.
Stop waiting.
It's done.
You know it.
It's you that needs
to let go.
To move on.
To breathe.
One last time.
Breathe in and release.
The pain.
The hurt.
The guilt.
The confusion.
The heartbreak.
Let it go.
It's over.
Move on.
Today.

Job Well Done

You were sent here
to break me.
To damage me.
To destroy my heart.
And you served your purpose
completely.
You became my inspiration.
The reason I could write.
Because in the pain
I had to find myself
to discover who I really was
inside.
In order to become whole
and not just a close half
of who I was supposed to be.
Yes.
Your purpose was to destroy me.
To leave me so wide open
that I'd have to fight through
my broken-
ness
through my mental mess.
It was the only route
to my greatness.
And you my friend...
fulfilled your purpose.
One day I'll be grateful.

Etched in Stone

That one time
he made love to me
for the first time...
Amazing.
He was amazing.
It was amazing.
Love was amazing.
I hope I never forget
The feeling.
The moment.
The taste.
The love.
The memory.
I hope my heart clings to it
and protects it...
forever.

Differences

We were so different.
Not from different places
but from different spaces...
mentally.
Both hustlers...
Me… Legally.
Him… By Any Means...
Necessary.
Him...
Bred in the Hood.
Me...
Forced to stay
in the house
so I was good.
While he was out
I could only stare out
of the window.
So dreaming is all I'd know.
And it's what protected me
and motivated me
to see the dreams
he couldn't see.
And even when I wanted us
to be...
Maybe we just couldn't.
Maybe we were too different.

Always Nothing

I gave you
the most valuable
and vulnerable
parts of me.
You didn't deserve it.
Weren't even worth it.
You don't know
treasure when you see it.
Can't accept love
when you need it.
I tried to make you worth it.
Made myself less observant
of your flaws...
Overlooked it all.
Until you looked over me.
Proved to me
that we would always be...
Nothing.

If Only

If you were still here
I'd tell you
I just wanted your love.
Perfectly imperfect.
I just wanted it.
Unconditional.
Permanent.
Consistent.
I needed it.
If you were still here
I'd tell you
You don't have to be perfect.
You just have to be around.
To show up.
To support.
To love in return.
I needed it.
If you were still here
I'd tell you
I had some bad relationships.
Some broken hearts.
Some hurt feelings.
Some fake friendships...
I needed you.
Around.
To protect me.
To love me.
Unconditionally.

It's time.

Constant.
Consistent.
Reminders.
It's time.
To let go.
Of you.
No questions.
No answers.
No closure.
No need.
It's time.
That's clear to me.
Goodbye love.

Empty Words

I don't trust
because feelings change.
I'm in love with you today...
But tomorrow...
Acting strange.
So I don't trust.
Because I fall for the
"I Love Yous"
And the "I need you in my lifes'"
And then I'm left
to piece together
the pieces
of everything broken inside.
Because I tried.
And because I trusted.
Empty words
rehearsed promises
they all lead to tears
and painful memories
my heart has difficulty
escaping.
So let's refrain from making...
More memories
and speaking...
More empty words.

Active Imagination

Trying to move forward
yet I keep looking back.
I miss him.
My heart is breaking and
I don't even know where he's at.
Where he buried that love
he showed me.
Where he hid that man.
Not sure where or why he buried
his amazing
don't think I will ever understand.
He wanted to be more
than just my friend.
and now...
He's damn near non-existent.
Not sure he ever really existed.
It was probably just my imagination.

36.

You've taught me
some of the greatest lessons
life has to offer.
For every smile I've smiled
I've cried one hundred tears.
For every day I hid the pain
you brought the effects
out from over the years.
For every time someone
told me they loved me
you gave me a day full of doubt.
I've learned the greatest lessons
with you...
Yet I still can't figure you out.
In you I found the purest joy
but also the deepest pain.
I reached a level of love
unknown by most
But I damn near drowned
in your rain.
I found myself looking
beneath my surface
only to discover none of those scars
ever healed.
So I fought and fought to love
my imperfections
that you just constantly chose to reveal.
It's been real.
You have taught me to
choose self-love first
so I've learned to dig within.
You have clouded my vision
but have shown me how to feel
and accept love through friendships
again.
It's like you're breaking yet fixing me
This time building me to last.
I'd be lying If I said you weren't amazing
but I'm looking forward to you being my past.
36.

Tears of Love

I feel the tears forming
because baby...
I'm in love
and I can't let go.
Even when I can't
let anyone know.
Even when I can't
let my feelings show.
I'm still in love.
I feel the tears forming.
Trying to hide...
What resides deep inside
the love buried
under the lies.
Deep in my soul
is where he resides.
Baby...
I'm in love.

Love The Real

Deep
Passionate
True
It's how I want to
love myself
believe in myself
support myself.
I want to love the parts of me
that others are too afraid
to touch
to look at
to keep.
I want to love
the parts of me that shine
so bright
that others are too afraid
to look at directly
because their hearts and minds
respect me.
I want to love the good
and the bad.
The perfect
and the imperfect.
Everything April is,
was, and desires to be...
That's what I want
to love.

The Point

My heart knows
real from fake
truth from lies
It recognizes
the feelings.
The vibes.
It knows
what makes it whole
and what breaks it.
Even when it's afraid
it tries again.
To hold on.
To open up.
To fight for what's within.
It always knows the truth
and it holds on to what's real.
For what would be the point of living
if you couldn't love...
If your heart couldn't feel?
If your heart wasn't willing?

Contact List

The funny thing is
I changed the name
over and over
even when nothing
really changes.
Sometimes I can bear
reality
and others
just what I wish he could be.
So I pick and I choose
to win or to lose.
Whatever makes me happy
at that moment.
Sometimes I'm hopeful
but sometimes I quit
I let love bloom
and I get rid of it
and move on.
But conversation or not
communication or none
I constantly change the names
to move on.

One Day

One day
you will look
and not cry.
One day
you will clearly see
the truth
and not be hurt by it.
Not doubt your worth
because of it.
Not have to re-evaluate
based on it.
One day
just like the others
you will "like"
and keep scrolling
your heart
won't keep trolling.
You'll be over it.
And you'll have everything
you need...
You'll have the truth.
And you'll be grateful.

It's Locked

I knocked on the door
so many times.
It wouldn't open.
Because of the effort
I was broken.
Always hoping
that he'd open his heart.
Give us a start
and not just an ending...
We were always ending.
Even when there was never
a clear beginning.
But I loved him.
And I'm sure that will always
be the case
I just can't fight
to be in his space.
Especially if the door
won't open.

Stay Human

My job
requires me to be numb.
Not dumb.
Just absent of feeling.
So I don't require healing
because the intake is a mess.
So much
that I can't process...
Any of it.
I just let it roll off of my mind
like rain
on rain boots
It's much too risky
to analyze and accept the truth.
So pretending it doesn't
really exist
is what I do.
It's how I survive
and still thrive
from the inside.
It's how I stay sane
and prevent myself from feeling
any pain
stops my mind from feeling
too strange.
And manages to keep me human.

CORE.

As we peel back the layers
of who I am at my core
I begin to feel raw
and unsure.
Not certain who I am…
Anymore.
Pain stacked on top
of pain.
No real healing
just band aids.
Just places where the pain
had been.
No healing just raw
skin.
The scars have lived so deep within
me
and the demons there
aren't friendly.
They are vicious
and hungry
They want all of my happiness
and sanity.
Their goal is simply to damage me.
Permanently.
But fortunately
God has a greater plan for me.

CHOSEN

I might have waited
my entire life
to be chosen.
To be protected.
Respected.
Loved.
I waited my entire life.
To be the one
who was chosen...
Just because.
I remember the younger version
of me.
Never secure.
Never sure.
Always dreaming.
But never chosen.
Never protected.
Always felt a little...
Neglected.
It was the small decisions
that left me lonely.
I just wanted to be loved...
not the only
One.
Just one of the chosen ones.

Closure.

This time
I just want closure
I want the reason.
Initially
I didn't think I'd need it.
But now I do.
I deserve it too.
I deserve the truth.
Don't want years to pass by
again
and still be confused.
Don't want to be wondering
if any of it was true.
I want to move on
with the entire truth
so I need closure.

Dazed In Love

From his name
to his walk
to his smile
I'm in love
with him.
His personality
his demeanor
his being
all of it.
I'm in love
with him.
Nothing material.
It's his energy
his love
his heart…
All the things money can't buy
create the numerous reasons why
I'm in love with him.

Rehab

Sometimes the knowing
is what hurts the most
trying to let go
of something so real
efforts to forget
what I feel
and heal...
Maybe.
He was my baby.
His memory
is one that resides deep
in my soul.
The only time in life
where I actually felt
whole.
Complete.
Healed.
Alive.
Alert.
The time when all of the pain
was finally worth
it.
That's what his presence did.
And without him...
I have to learn
to heal the pain
on my own
fill the hole
all alone.
Learn to be strong.
And happy.

Next.

He doesn't exist.
I've decided.
I tried it.
Blindly.
I trusted.
With both feet
I jumped in
Just wanted him.
But he proved to me
repeatedly
that a we
just couldn't be
Because he didn't want it
enough
He didn't love me
enough
so I have to love me
enough
to move on.

Sun, Moon, Stars

He was everything
beautiful and amazing
but unreachable.
Everything that you admire
but can't touch.
Can't hold.
Can't keep.
He was all of those things.
The kind that make you smile.
Warm your heart.
Heal your soul.
He was the type
to make you feel whole.
Or safe.
Or at peace.
He was that kind of amazing.
The kind where you could bask
in the beauty of everything he was...
His smile.
His conversation.
His love.
He was like everything
you'd admire from afar...
He was equivalent
to the sun, the moon, and the stars.

Drop The Beat

I got flows
Yep yep
I do
I can write about love
and flow about life too.
The highs
The lows
The pimps
and the hoes...
Just kidding!
But I really could
I believe my flows
are just that good.
Write out your life
Get you out the hood
Help you dream
Make you fly
Find your magic
Then ask me why…
did I take so long
to unleash
these flows...
You weren't ready.
Just so you know.

List Of Amazing

I could literally list
all the reasons
he's amazing.
But the more reasons
that fill these pages,
the less amazing I want him
to be.
He doesn't belong to me
Even though he belongs
with me.
He's not too blind to see.
He knows and has lived
the same history.
He's forever connected
to me.
One day I'm hoping
we will be.
Until then...
The list of amazing things
will have to cease.

Loved Late

I remember the first time
I heard my mom
say she loved me...
as an adult.
After I almost
had a physical altercation
with a sister...
Situation.
Suddenly
I remembered
all the times
I felt neglected
not because she wasn't there
my heart just never felt
respected.
And me...
Never felt protected.
I always felt alone.
Forced to face my thoughts
and fears on my own
as a child.
I always felt like the battle
was all mine
Praying it would pass
in time.
And that real love would find
my heart.
I guess this was just a part
of being child #3
with a single mom
just trying to make ends meet.
I know first hand
the feeling of defeat
So I never forgot
that moment.
But I still wish
it was from a happier time.

Eyes On The Prize

I'm going to press forward
even when I can't see the staircase.
I'm still going to climb
one step at a time.
Because they believe in me
and I believe in me.
They just don't know
it's the staircase
that I can't see.
But that won't stop me from walking
from constantly talking
from fighting for my greatness
I know that God made this
and He's got this.
Watch this.
❤

Truth About the Night

Sometimes I lay in the bed at night
and think about him.
His love...
His ways...
He was such a powerful passing phase.
I cried for days
trying to get over him.
Erase the memories
of knowing him.
All the things I hoped
to be showing him.
I prayed that I'd forget
or the thoughts would no longer hurt.
Pain so bad
I almost forgot my worth.
I don't know what's worse,
not knowing
or knowing so much
that now you can't forget.
Can't erase
what you don't regret.
The memories buried
so deep inside
the love engrained
so the tears I hide.
I'll love him forever
of that,
I'm sure
but I just can't hold on to the hurt anymore.

WALLS

She builds walls
around her
Not so you can break them down
but so she can hide her
where nobody can find her
the real version
She doesn't believe
anyone is really worth it
The authentic version
is like a hidden treasure
not for your entertainment
or your pleasure
Alone she battles the weather
behind the walls
built with brick
so they never fall
and when her emotions
are hidden
It's easier for her to stand tall
so don't climb
just let her hide
she's safe there
until she decides...
You're worth it.

Open Wounds

I've tried to fix so many
broken people.
And I've been cut
so many times
by the broken pieces.
Still my heart needs it.
Needs to see it.
Their happiness.
I long to see the magic
in others.
Not just lovers,
But friends...
And family.
But sometimes it damages me.
Trying to get them to their happy,
trying to get them to see
their light is what the world needs
and I need them to be free.
To come shine with me...
In the darkness.

The Root

Sometimes we have to dig
deeper.
The problem
is not always residing
on the surface.
Sometimes it's deeper.
And to fix it,
You have to be willing
to go the distance
to dig it up
to face it head on
to bring back
what's gone.
To fix it,
You have to be real
to feel what you feel
to cry, scream, and heal.
You have to be willing
to pull back the veil
to fight through your hell
and sometimes to tell...
Your story.
That's how you fix it.

Unguarded

I don't know that I will ever
again
be unguarded.
I tried it.
My world fell apart.
The damage done to my heart...
Unimaginable.
Couldn't even pull myself out
of the pain long enough
to save me
and my happy.
It was like I was drowning
in my own tears.
Years of fears
reasons now clear
Those walls served a purpose.
Whoever brought them down
should have been worth it
would have to deserve it...
Me.
In my authenticity.
Raw.
Bare.
They would really have to care.
Deeply.
On a level never before seen.
Man of my DREAMS
type shit.
Yes, that's it.
He basically doesn't even exist.
You won't catch me unguarded.
Again.

Picket Fences

The truth is
Picket fences don't exist.
Happily ever after...
Movies only.
Highlight reels on social media
will have your
#relationshipgoals
based on things that are phony.
People not alone,
but still lonely.
The reality is,
there's no "typical" reality.
People are not in love
or they are...
But a picture or a post
never provides what's really
in a heart.
Some things are good
from the start...
Others, when they part.
Love is like... Art.
Completely dependent upon
your interpretation.

Love's Truth

One day I know...
Just like I hope...
Like my heart desires
Like the part
That takes you higher
We will be.
One.
Us.
Because that lwhat love does.
It comes back each time.
It falls back in line.
It eases your mind.
Only this time,
Love will stay.
For good.

TRUE. LOVE.

There's an amazingness
that is true love
Many people
think they've felt it.
Have known it.
True love isn't basic.
You don't get over it
Move on past it
Let go of it.
It buries itself
in your being.
Penetrates your heart.
Controls your mind.
True love doesn't
let go.
It holds on for dear life.
Screams.
Cries.
Fights.
It holds on for life.
And when it's bright
It's amazing!
Euphoric.
Mind blowing.
Eye opening.
Thought provoking.
True love
is when your happiness
is to a level
in which no words
can explain
No hands can reach
No teacher can teach.
True love is the cure
to everything.
To hurt
To pain
To heartbreak
To rain.
It's the sanity
in your insane.
True love brings change
Heals pain
Stops blame.
It changes you.
And when you find it,
You'll know it. ❤

Options

I would love
To touch him.
Rub his skin
I remember him
The details...
Big and small
His strength
Him..
Big and tall.
My heart makes him perfect
Even when I know he's flawed.
I would love to hold him
To rub him
To feel him
To love him.
To make love to him
Share sweat with him
Create more memories
Conquer regret with him.
To hold him
Squeeze him
Taste him
Please him.
Be free with him
Be me with him
Forget all of my needs
With him.
At this point I'd even accept
Conversation.

All Love

This is who I am.
Love.
I live
And breathe...
Love.
I eat
Speak
And think...
Love.
With every breath
And every hope
It's what I believe in...
Love.
Every thought
Of every second
Of every day...
It's love.
My motivation
My dedication
My inspiration...
Forever...
LOVE.

Sometimes

Sometimes you just want
the love to be real
to help you feel
or to ease the pain.
Sometimes you just want
the love
to be the sane
in your insanity
to protect you
and set you free
to hold you
when you feel
the need.
Sometimes you just want
the love
to be what it promised
it would be.
Around forever
or as soon as you need
it.
Sometimes you just want
love to be
exactly what you thought
it was
in the beginning.

Fragile State Of Mind

Feeling extra fragile
these days…
Breakable.
Everything matters to me.
Even the smallest things.
Everything.
Matters.
To.
Me.
Every feeling.
Every kind word.
Every hurtful one.
Every compliment.
Every hug.
Everything.
Even silence.
The positive kind
and the negative.
They both speak volumes
to my heart
And right now.. I'm fragile.

End of the Day

At the end of the day
the one person
I would do anything
to hold on to
let go of me first.
When things began
to go wrong
and life stopped going right
It was me
who was left with questions
at night.
It was me who didn't know
if things were wrong
or still right.
It was me in the dark.
Me with the broken heart.
Me drying my tears.
Me alone after all these years.
At the end of the day
when life needed to be adjusted
I was your first adjustment...
You would have been my last.

What's More Amazing?

The world may not be focused
on love
but for some reason
my life revolves around it.
My soul can't breathe
without it
my heart doesn't beat without it.
Not sure how the world survives
each day,
When I can barely
get away
without mentioning the word.
It's the best thing
I've ever heard of
the greatest feeling
I've ever felt.
Is there anything else?
What's more amazing than love?

Little Girls

For all of the little girls
who have been violated
and all of the women
whose lives have been changed
by someone familiar
or strange...
I see you.
For the little girls
who have just become afraid
and the moms and dads
who know they regularly prayed
for peace and understanding
for healing and for hope...
God hears you.
And He knows.
It's just the world that's in denial.
The people who would prefer to blame the child
instead of seeking help for the one
who started it all
instead of stopping more innocent people
from the fall...
Even when they believe you.
The denial will never
make things okay
It will never heal your heart
or make the pain go away
So you have to find strength
to be strong and be bold.
This world is a place
where people turn cold.
But remember your reactions
are always by choice
So don't ever let someone silence
Your voice...
Like I did.

Oblivious

I've been trying
to make myself forget
the happiness I felt
the love deep inside
the way I allowed myself
to be free
eliminated my pride
for love.
Living in the truth
made life even better
like I could brave the storm
as long as we were together.
Actually
there was no storm
when we were together
Because the world didn't even exist...
Not when I hugged him
or those moments
when we kissed.
We were the only living beings
I could see
I'm just not sure
what happened to him… or me.

Witness

He watched me die inside.
He loved me
but not enough
to make the sacrifice
that would save me.
So he listened
to my cries
and my pleas
and did...
Nothing.
He heard me though.
Not even sure
if he was affected
by the damage
that was occurring
to my heart
and my soul...
He left a gaping hole.
And because of the pain
I became whole.
On my own.

You Have to Know

You have to know
who you are.
Because when you're crying
inside
God is the only one
who hears you...
And he already knows.
He is aware of the Blessing
and the greatness
that is you.
He's just waiting
for you to recognize
your truth.
So you have to know
and be certain
So whenever you're down
or you're hurting
your worth won't be lost
in the downfall of it all.

Writing Open

For the first time
I don't want to write.
Writing makes me think.
Makes me feel.
Deeply.
Evaluate
Thoroughly.
Makes me tell the truth.
Writing opens up my heart
spills everything inside
and then seals it
without protecting it
with my pride.
Writing makes me bare...
Full body and mind
Revealed
Writing breaks me open
and then attempts to heal
me from the inside.
It's like surgery
for my mind
and my heart.
Like canvas waiting
on paint
to become art.
This writing...
It's the only way I can cope.
Willing or not.

SOONER

The sooner you understand
that life will happen
with or without you
the sooner you will commit
to live.
The sooner you realize
that the world still smiles
when your heart is broken
the harder you will work
to move forward.
The sooner you learn
that you can't make other people
love you
the sooner you will cry it out
and learn to love yourself.
The sooner you allow your pain
to surface, your tears to fall, and
your wounds to heal...
The sooner you can be real...
With yourself.

Anyway

I tell myself not to write
and I do that shit anyway.
Tell myself not to feel
and I feel anyway.
I tell myself just to chill
and I text you to reveal
that I'm not as patient
as I want to be
that I'm struggling
without you next to me
that I'm fighting myself
to be strong for you
and it's making me doubt
if your love is true…
Even though I thought it was.
I'm messing myself up for love!

Baby Girl… He's Been Gone

If you never pick up the phone
to call him again
you will never hear his voice.
If you decide against sending
that text message
you will never know
if he'll respond.
You're so busy
holding on
that you're carrying
this "friendship" all alone
Baby girl, he's been gone.
Why are you still holding on?

Star Gazing

I stared at him
while he was sleeping.
Amazed that he was real
and in my presence.
Sleeping.
I couldn't.
Didn't want to waste time
with my eyes closed.
He was real.
Next to me.
Loving me.
I watched him
like people
admire treasure
and unusual beauty.
But he was human.
My love.
He was my heart.

The Writing

I have to write
to stay sane.
These words are like an umbrella
in the pouring rain.
Protection when danger is lurking.
A slow pace
when the miracles are working
and I need to be patient.
I have to write
to stay in a good head space
to fill the hurt and anger
with fresh happiness on my face.
It's healing
and soothing
and such a relief to my soul
reminds me that even when I break
I'm still whole.
It's the writing.

My Heart Remembers

There were so many times
when I wanted to call him.
Pick up the phone...
Hear his voice.
Then I remember
the day he stopped
answering
or calling back.
My heart remembers that.
I even consider sending
a text.
A "Hey, how are you?"
to see what he says.
But then I remember
the days it took him hours
just to respond...
My heart remembers that.
It remembers the waiting
the response creating
the sadness deep inside
the "Damn! Why. did. I... text him?"
and not being able
to take the feelings back.
My heart remembers that.
So it refuses to let me
try again.

Never Chase

One day he woke up
and realized he was good…
without me.
And that's okay.
But My heart and soul
got the message
late.
My mind...
Caught on right away.
Tell the others
we can't make him stay...
Nor do we want to.
Love sets you free
even when it hurts.
Let's cry the tears
but never forget our worth...
We know what we deserve.
Just like the other times
we'll battle through the pain.
We'll sleep a little longer
but eventually,
we will dance in the rain!
We'll hold close the memories
for they brought so much joy...
But we shall NEVER
chase after a boy!

Misunderstood

People might think I'm crazy...
The way I feel about love.
The great ones usually are...
Misunderstood.
And I'm definitely great
at love.
Hopelessly romantic.
I believe in it all.
Love at first sight…
Romance...
Being down for the fall...
into love
that is.
It's always worth it.
The way it takes your breath away,
gives you life,
helps you live.
I'm all the way down
for love.
Would give my last breath for it.
Spend my last dollar on it.
Sacrifice my...
Time for it.
Love is everything.
It changes everything.
Fixes everything.
HEALS EVERYTHING.
But people might think
I'm crazy...
The way I feel about love.
The great ones
usually are...
Misunderstood.

ALL

I'm way too fly
to have a breaking heart.
Love is good
for tearing the good ones apart.
I believed in our love
from the start
and now I can't stop
the bleeding from my heart.
I believed him.
Trusted him.
Let down all my walls.
I let him in.
Confided in him.
Gave him the key
to it all.
My heart.
My love.
My thoughts
deep inside.
I fought for him.
Loved him hard.
Completely let go of my pride.
No lie.
I gave it all to him
in its truest form.
Never had I done that before…
Just not my norm.
But it was all or nothing
this time around
I wasn't willing to risk
putting my love back
in the lost and found.
He was the truth
so I gave him the crown...
He walked away
with that shit.

EVERYTHING

His smile is everything.
Today he smiled.
Told me he loved mine...
But I fell in love with his
a long time ago.
He is EVERYTHING.

Broken Insides

We die inside
until there's no more room
for dead bones
to live in our bodies.
Trying to please
other people
and satisfy societies
limits and boxes.
Trying to uphold
our images and reputations
We die slowly...
Trying to fit in.
Trying to make friends.
Dying.
To pretend.
But somewhere we must
find ourselves and live in our truth
chase the dreams
and commit to the innocence
we had in our youth.
We have to be true to ourselves
and the fire
that burns within.
Be true to what satisfies
our soul
completes us...
Makes us whole.
Makes us happy.
We must commit
to that.
To shining our light.
To living and breathing
and sharing...
Our truth.
So there are less dead bones
in our bodies.

Happily Never After

I have to pretend
the kind of love we have
only exists in fairytales.
That what we felt
was all in a dream
that God allowed me
to dream fully.
I have to pretend
that the way I felt
was just something
people read about in
books...
My imagination
is the only way
I can survive your absence.
Because if I allow myself
to believe it was real
and allow myself
to feel what I feel
my happiness
will come crashing down
the tears will fall
simply at the sound...
of your voice
or your name being mentioned
I was never able
to keep your attention.
What I thought
was forever
was simply a temporary thing
something to help you
pass the time
while you were debating...
and then you walked away.
So the safest place
for the memories
to stay
is in my imagination.
That place where
Happily Ever Afters
were created
and true love never ends
with either person devastated.
I will forever pretend
it was all a dream...
A beautiful one.
But it had to end
because I woke up.

Urgency

Everything is urgent
to me.
I'm not sure there is anything
in life
that I can wait on...
Debate on...
I'm not the one.
My patience
is thin
almost non-existent.
If there was a class on that
I definitely missed it.
I want everything now
I will do whatever it takes
I want the outcome
and I'm down
to put in the work
with no breaks.
I'm that chick.
But I'm worth it
you'll see
because I'm not sure
there is anything in life
that isn't urgent to me.

Save it.

I'm fine.
I'm really just pretending though.
How can I ever really
let it go...
I don't know.
Day by day
is how I plan to take it
That's the only way
I think I'll make it.
For now...
The plan is really just to fake it.
All I can do is reside
in denial
the love's too deep
to not be worthwhile.
It's like my air was suddenly
restricted
like someone pulled me over
and gave me a ticket
towed my car
and made me walk
I die inside
when we don't talk.
I just want him
but I'm calling it quits.
Love is so full of shit!

I LOVE MYSELF

(Written at 11 years old)

I love myself.
Young, Black, Bold, and Beautiful.
I love myself.
Intelligent, aggressive, and enthusiastic.
I love myself.
My book sense and my common sense
that helps me just say no
to the distractions in society today
that are trying to hold me back.
I love myself
when I sing like the birds
on a spring morning
and dance like a gazelle having fun.
Thinking to myself,
I will always be number one.
I love myself
my stubbornness,
my attitudes,
and knowing what goals I have in life
and how to achieve them.
I love myself and what I see.
I love myself
because I know
I'm just being me.

Still Love?

Just not sure anymore
No excitement
like before
Innocence... gone
Stole the pure happiness
we were vibing on.
Life came in
and took its toll.
Took that half
and I'm still whole
but I'm broken.
Not sure if I'm in pieces
or just a little cracked
What I wouldn't give
to get my baby back...
This is wack.
I don't even know
where we are at.
I'm not even sure
what this is...
Or if I should hold on...
Still love?
Or all gone?

Stuck in Denial

Been in denial
for so long...
Trying my best to hold on
to his words
when actions are always
what I need.
Words are like bringing water
to a feed...
Where only actions let you eat.
I've been in denial...
No. I've been in trust
because I knew this was real love
and not lust.
It was the words
I had to believe
when the actions
started to deceive.
Or did I have that mixed up...
Should I not even give a fuck?
Was it the actions
I should believe
and the words I should question?
Or should I hold on to whichever
part doesn't leave me guessing?
Am I missing the lesson?
Been trying my best...
To hold on...
I've been in denial too long.

Empty For Certain

I want to write
but tonight...
I'm feeling empty.
Both Love and pain
motivate me.
But right now...
I don't even know what I'm feeling
Not sure if I'm breaking
or healing.
Do I cry?
Or celebrate?
Is this what love is?
Or is this the feeling of hate?
I just don't know anymore...
Feeling empty for sure.

Chapter 12.

I have a million feelings
to give him
He's currently closed...
Closed off.
Leaving me wondering,
Is love lost?
He says it's not
but words and actions...
Two different things.
These days
you gotta DO
what you mean.
And since he's not
doing anything...
I'm doing me.
Chapter 12 of 12.

Anything for Love

Yep.
I'd give him anything.
Everything.
That's what love is worth.
Everything.
Whatever it wants.
He wants...
I want...
LOVE wants.
I'd give love everything.

Don't Chance It

I think I just want to write
because I don't understand...
How can you love someone
And be ALL in
and then...
Barely a friend.
No time to text
or call or chill
No time to love
to listen
to build.
I don't get it.
How do you not make the sacrifice
when your heart wants to hold on?
Why would someone risk
a true love
being gone?

Privacy

I could write about him
all day
but I need to do that shit
in private.
People wouldn't understand
the way I love him...
Crave him.
Need him.
The way my body knows
when he's near
and struggles when he leaves.
The way he unknowingly
raises my frequency.
They wouldn't understand.
How even when buried
the feelings wouldn't leave.
Almost committed myself to therapy.
But now
even when the distance hurts
I don't want to get over him
I never want to get over him.
He is my happy....
The organic version.
He makes the pain and the trials
worth it.
He makes life everything
that people wish for... dream for
He is that "more" that people long for
He is that happily ever after
people read about in fairytales.
He's my air...
But the world is so unaware...
So I gotta write about this shit...
in private.

Drunk Thoughts

I will always remember the day
I got drunk
because love walked away.
When I was sober
it talked its way
into my life.
Made me want be its wife.
I would have given up
my nights,
these rights
to make it right.
It was all right...
Until it wasn't.
So I had a drink
or a dozen.
Trying to erase
the pain of the heartbreak
The heartaches
Drinking...
Doing whatever it takes
to get rid of the memories
of him and me.
He was never a friend to me.

The Real Thing

It was the most perfect love
Ever.
So perfect that words
will never accurately
describe its power.
I've seen people in love before
It was much stronger than that.
It was true.
It was innocent
It should have been forever
but life didn't want us together
or maybe it was him.
And maybe it was game.
And maybe I was lame.
Or insane.
But whatever it was,
It was definitely the most perfect love
I have ever felt.
Or seen.
It was the real thing.

Can't Be

I won't ever be in denial
again.
While he's just my friend
he's not just a friend.
Never been.
My heart won't let it end
my heart won't mend
the feelings are real
I won't deny the way I feel
I won't hide what I know is true
I won't punish myself
to hide the truth.
It was real.
Every second
Every I love you
Every look
Every hug
Every touch
It was love.
The real kind.
The kind you could still see
if you were blind.
He was all mine
in those moments.
We know it.
He showed it.
And because of that
my heart won't let it end
my heart won't mend
he'll never just be my friend
I won't ever be in denial again.

Resurrection

He woke me up.
Mind. Body. Soul.
Made me realize I was
pretending.
I wasn't whole.
He touched me
in places no human
could ever go.
His presence took control.
Put my life in a choke hold.
Rearranged all I thought I was
and could be...
Elevated me
and then set me free.
Blindly.
I was lost and could no longer
find me.
The old me...
Gone.
Don't even remember what she looks like,
felt like, or what she thought...
What she taught.
She was gone... changed.
Everything rearranged
because he had the power
to awaken me.
And the willingness to walk away.

His Loss

I could've loved him...
Right.
Like all night.
I wanted him to be my...
Future.
But he couldn't act right.
I was willing...
To rearrange my life...
For him
Give up my rights
for him.
He wasn't wit' it though.
Didn't get it...
No.
Or maybe I was too much...
For him
to handle.
Still no other woman
will ever hold a candle
to me.
His loss.

Motivation

It is the sadness that motivates me.
The anger and the heartbreak
are the reason
I'm here.
The flame is LIT
by the pain.
Motivated by the forced change.
Writing to prevent myself
from going insane.
I have an overactive brain.
Passionate about love,
peace, and respect
but sometimes I gotta keep my mind in check.
It wants to love AND protect.
It wants to live without neglect.
In retrospect....
It just wants to be understood
To be loved...
Real good.
And not just for motivation.

Sorry

At the end of the day
love just isn't enough.
You need action.
Respect.
Chemistry.
You need the "extras"
that make you want to be...
In love.
Be one.
Feel whole.
Because love itself,
just isn't enough.
Sorry.

What's Understood

It's love.
I didn't get it.
I do now.
It's clear.
Doesn't need an explanation.
Doesn't require discussing
the situation.
We know
exactly what it is.
Exactly who we are.
Exactly what we mean...
To each other.

Reasons Why

Sometimes I die inside.
My heart breaks
and so does my pride.
I'd open it up
and let the rain wash it away
if I could.
I'd trade the pain
for the good.
Sometimes my heart breaks
inside.
Still pumps blood
but I know it died.
It needs love. True Love
to survive.
It's my reason... why.
And sometimes even after
the sadness and the pain
the sun follows the storm
creates rainbows after the rain
Sometimes it's proof
that I can live again.
And that's my reason why.

A While

I miss him
It would be a lie
If I said I didn't.
His smell
His touch
His smile...
It's been a while.
Haven't even seen his face
Heard his laugh
Been the cause of his smile...
Damn.
It's been a while.

Soul Mate

His love speaks
to my soul.
I didn't even know
that was possible.
I didn't know my soul
was yearning
until he showed up
and loved me.
It changed me.
Rearranged me.
Made me feel
like we made it to heaven's gates.
He was my soul mate.

Breaking Point

You know you're at the breaking point
when the things you once loved
don't love you back.
When your happiness feels all out
of whack
and nothing seems to get you back on track.
When the tears
that have been forming finally
find a way to fall
but you're completely alone
so there's no comfort at all.
I'm there.
Broken heart
Broken dreams
and I still care
But my effort bucket
is almost bare.
I have no more to give
no more love
no more fight
I don't care what's wrong
or right.
This is about all I can take...
Before I reach that point where I break.

Roller Coaster

My heart
is on an emotional roller coaster.
Is it love?
Is it not?
Are we cold?
Or are we hot?
Are we a thing?
Or are we not?

Repeat

I'd be broken
If I lost him.
Again.
Lost.
Hurt.
Damaged.
Frozen.
Numb.
Extremely dumb.
I'd be torn.
Thrown.
Betrayed.
Dismayed.
Love dead
Not just delayed.
I'd be full of rage.
Or pain.
But mostly hurt.
Heart completely broken
and buried in the dirt.
Negative balance
on my worth.
If I lost him again.

No Replacement

I could talk to hundred people
laugh a hundred times
crack a hundred smiles
and I'd still be missing you.
Nothing fills the space...
Nothing takes your place
when you're gone.

Love is Dope.

Love is dope.
Or crack.
Or meth...
Definitely a drug.
Your life will change
if you are overcome by love.
It's no easy fix.
It's not simple to move on.
It's not one of those feelings
you ignore until it's gone.
Love is a drug.
I've done the research.
The endorphins it releases
will have your mind, heart, and your feelings hurt.
It blinds you.
Gives you a high
that no rehab can cure
and should you ever fall
the pain will be a lot to endure.
So proceed with caution.
Think it out before giving in.
It's impossible to fight it,
Love always wins.

Leveled

Want to celebrate the highs
and the lows
until the highs
get too low.
It's the hurt
that hurts too much
to show.
It's the moving on
that causes pain...
You know?
It's the thoughts
in the brain
that make the emotions
show
The pain of letting go...
It's too much
You know?
It's the moving on
again
that's sad
It's the been there
done that makes me mad.
It's the repetition
of the disappointment
that makes me question
it all
It's never the rise...
It's the fall.

The Fall

She told me that I was up so high
but that meant there was a long way
to fall.
She said be careful...
She was right.
I should've been careful
should have been guarded
should have been silent
should have been patient
should have just waited.
I was up so high...
Feels like I'm free falling
from the sky.
I could have waited.
Been careful.
Guarded...
But it was worth it.
The memories…
They are all worth the fall.

Waiting Room

I wait for him.
His presence.
His touch.
His love.
His voice.
I wait for it.
Impatiently.
But still waiting.
His presence is fresh air.
His face... pure joy.
His hugs... soul food.
His love... the key to everything
that's normally locked
inside of me.
He's always reviving me.
He doesn't even know it.
But I wait for him...
So I can breathe again.
Be alive again
Be me again.
He's so much more
than just a friend.

Tomorrow

Tomorrow is just not promised.
Today is really all we have.
All we get is now
to live, to love, to laugh.
This moment is all we get.
You either use it or lose it.
Literally.
Live
like there is no tomorrow.
The truth is,
there really might not be one.

That Day

There comes a day
when you'd rather be awake
than sleep.
A day when the good things
are happening
in real life
and not in your dream.
The days when you wake up
with excitement
looking forward to the day.
The one where the goodness
is flowing your way.
The days when your reality
is worth the work it takes
worth the time you've given
and the moves you have to make.
That day… It's worth it.

He is Love

If you could put a picture
next to "in love" in the dictionary
I'm sure it would be his.
He is love.
He is "in love"
He is the definition
of everything love is.
What it means
How it feels
What it does
How it respects
How it holds on
How it commits
How it protects
How it cares
He IS the definition
of how love reacts.
How it speaks
How it makes effort
How it comes back.
He IS love.
How it makes you feel
How it makes you think
How it makes you smile
How it makes you believe.
He is love
and Love is him.

Feelings

Feelings are for the birds.
Those things get you hurt.
Mind. Heart. Life.
DISTURBED.
Is it possible to give some away
and not have to take them back?
Like add to someone else's
feelings?
I'd be cool with that.
Caring deeply
is sometimes too much.
Yearning?
Crying?
Trying?
Caring?
I want no such.
Forget feelings.
You can have them.
Yours and mine too.
Gotta shake those feelings
before they destroy you.

I. Me. She. Her.

Internal Monologue

Sometimes
I just don't want to care
about anybody else
about anything else
but me.
I don't give a damn
about "social" media
Don't want to view
your highlight reel.
I really don't care
how you feel.
Not at this moment
Not later either
I'm worried about April
I. Me. She. Her.
That's it.
Concerning myself with you
creates bullshit.
Creates comparison
and judgement
and envy
and pain
turns some of the sunshine
I had
into rain.
Sometimes reminds me
that some things never change.
Increases my pain
my anguish
the strain.
Causes massive floods
when the prediction
was no rain.
That shit can drive
a healthy mind insane.
So I'm good.
Just worrying about me today.
Just concerned with
I. Me. She. Her.
That's what's best for sure.
So that's what I prefer.

Insecurities

I might still be
a little insecure.
Hella
unsure.
Afraid to trust.
To believe.
Is this really a real thing?
I might be a little afraid
it's too good to be true
when he looks into my eyes
and says "I love you."
I might just be scared
to believe and accept it.
Scared I might regret it.
Scared he might neglect it…
Me.
I'm scared to let my heart run free.
Scared to let it live on my sleeve.
I might just be a little insecure
in this situation.

Restoration

The chaos of the world
fell silent
the day he told me
he still loved me.
For years I cried
for him.
Died inside
missing him.
Filled a binder full
of poetry
loving him.
Years.
Decades actually.
Then one day
in the midst of chaos
and stress
and sadness
and emptiness
he appeared.
Suddenly
everything wrong
was right again.
Everything broken
was mended.
Sadness was happiness.
Stress had ended.
His love made me whole.
All of me.

Interference

The feelings from the past
are interfering with the present.
The loss
The heartbreak
The sadness
The uncertainty
The pain
of losing you.
Even though you're finally present
my heart is having difficulty
Repairing
Mending
Restarting
Trusting
It's like no matter how much love
is added
or given
or shared
Somewhere in there
It remembers
It cries
It screams
It starves
It yearns
It breaks...
For all of the time lost.
All of the pain felt.
All of the misunderstandings.
All of the aching.
All of the missing you
to the point that words could
no longer describe
the strength of the pain.
It was like death... to my heart
but my brain was still there.
Trying to process
how you could really not care
about me.

Love Him

I want to love him.
Protect his heart.
Make him feel safe.
I want to show him
the good.
All the things he should
have already experienced
and seen.
I want him to know how it feels
to be treated like a king.
I want to love him
the way his heart deserves
and his body needs.
I want to be his everything.
I really just want to love him.

Her.

I remember her.
The girl.
In high school.
The one who fell in love
and got scared.
Scared to feel.
Scared to care.
Scared to be in love.
Her.
I remember her.
Scared it would end.
Loving her "friend."
I remember her from back then
and I understand her...
Today.

No Feelings

I just want no feelings.
No love
No wanting to fall in love
No wanting to be in love
No caring about love
No sadness
No madness
NONE.
I would take some happy though.
Some elated
Some delighted
Some excited though.
I would take that.
I would make that.
The other stuff though...
I wanna escape that.
Wanna be numb to the fairy tales
and numb to the pain
numb to the I love yous
that didn't last for more than 10 days.
I wanna be numb to the anger
and numb to the lies
I want no tears falling from these eyes.
But give me the happy.
I'm ready for joy without the pain.
I'm ready for the world to help me re-focus.
Help me change.
Just no feelings.

Whole

I can't eat.
Or think.
Or concentrate.
I can't. Focus.
I can't.
The memories of last year
have become the memories
of yesterday.
Of this morning.
Of 5 minutes ago.
Instead of absence,
there is presence.
Instead of hurt,
there is forgiveness.
Instead of sadness,
there is truth.
And closure.
And opening.
And the end of the beginning.
This life cycle…
Simply Amazing.
And beyond our control.
Even when empty,
we are whole.

Puzzled

Puzzle complete.
Years of yearning
Weeks of wondering
Days of distance
Minutes of mystery
Seconds of sadness
Repeated cycle.
For decades.
When the last piece of the puzzle
goes missing
no where in sight
No life
No flight
No day
No night
No wrong
No right
It's missing.
And until it's found...
Incomplete will be the puzzle.

Remainder

Nothing is threatened here.
Real love can't be threatened, right?
No one interferes with that.
No one gets to step to bat.
Real love IS the home run.
The shooting of the starting gun.
The gold medal.
The finish line.
The first AND the last time.
It's the beginning and the end.
The "we can't just be friends."
Or is it the "even if we have to just be friends?"
It's the "I can't let you go even when I try."
The "my heart still wants to know why."
It's the butterflies on the inside.
Real Love.
It can't be threatened. Or altered. Or changed.
Love always remains.

My Heart

My heart is where the memories
are kept.
Where the experiences have slept.
Where the surface level
turns into depth.
My heart.
Where the feelings reside
and all the pain hides
Where the facades subside.
My heart.
The bearer of the hurt
and the pain
The guilt and the shame
The solace and the insane.
My heart.
Where the tears run like streams
Where the adult still has dreams
Where the sun shows its beams.
My heart.

Outlet to Freedom

I realize writing may be the only
effective outlet I have.
The only way I'm understood
The only way I find the freedom
of self-expression and honesty.
The only way to be free from judgement
and fear
and hurt.
This writing is the only way
to be free of pain.
Of heartbreak.
Of deceit.
Of anger.
It's the only outlet.
The only safe place to be me
To be free.
Completely.

Look For Love

We just look for love.
Wherever we find it
is where we plant our feet.
We hang onto the feeling.
The warmth.
The happiness.
We guard it.
Watch it.
Nurture it.
We just look for love.
To encourage us and protect us.
To support us and adore us.
Wherever we find it.
We hold on to it.
We fight for it.
We cry for it.
We yearn for it.
We just look for love.

It's Life

I've accepted the fact
that I may never see your face
Again.
Feel your warmth
Again.
Hear your voice...
Ever.
Again.
I've learned to accept it
while my heart breaks
back into
a million pieces.
I'm not even in need
of a reason.
I know what it is...
It's life.

It's Simple.

I love you.
Plain and simple.
It's situations and opinions
that complicate things.
My love knows
exactly what it is.
Exactly how it feels.
It's clear.
There is no confusion
that I love you.
It's not complicated.
It's simple but real.
I know exactly how I feel.
I love you.
My mind
My heart
My soul
All of it
Loves you.

In Your Presence

I could go insane
thinking of you.
I just want to be
in your presence.
Breathe the air you breathe.
See the same sun and stars
in the sky
that you see.
See the same cars passing by
on the street.
I just want to smell
your aroma.
Watch your chest move
up and down
as you inhale the city's air.
I want to see the waves in your hair.
Up close.
Personal.
I want to be in your space.
I want to live there.
Be there.
Sleep there.
I want to breathe your air.
Hear your voice.
Feel your warmth.
Experience your love.
In your presence.

Memories Souled

She's holding on to memories
decades old.
Coffee once burning hot
Now cold.
Now old.
Memories…
They live deep.
So deep that they surpassed her heart and mind.
They reside in her soul.
Guarded with a passcode
that only love can open.
The kindred soul has spoken.
It's the key to the lock.
The protection
that guards the block
of memories
deep in her soul.

Memory In A Bottle

I'd wrap your memory in a bottle if I could.
Gather all the good.
Seal it tight with a written reminder.
If lost,
Don't hesitate to find her...
Me.
Don't be afraid to be free.
Don't wait on thee
and don't deny the need.
I'd wrap in the bottle the taste of your lips.
The movement of my hips...
When I know you're watching.
I'd seal it with your scent...
That heavy, well washed shirt
that smelled of Tide Detergent.
I'd preserve it.
You were worth it.
ARE.
Worth.
It.
I'd preserve it.
For days. Years. Decades. For life.
I should have been your wife.
But instead...
I'll wrap your memory in a bottle
because I can.
Because this love understands
soul ties never end.
Like your memory
in this bottle.

You Can't Change Love

You can't change love.
You have no right to move
on without it
to move past
without acknowledging it
to press mute on its voice.
You can't change love.
You can try to hide its beauty
but its light shines through
the darkness.
Its power heals. Mends. Saves.
Its presence changes. It shocks. It stays.
You can't change love
and you have no right to move on without it.

Forever

It was that day.
The one I remembered.
I loved him.
My mind moved on.
My heart suppressed.
My soul reminded…
We are forever.

Life Goes On

Life goes on for everyone
even when yours stops.
Even when daily circumstances
cause your heart to drop.
Life goes on
and time still passes
while you attempt to get back on track.
It's time that waits for no one.
It's time that we never get back.
Life goes on for everyone
and eventually
life will go on for you.
Stay focused
and always give your best.
Your life is your truth.

Write You Away

Your memory is a
burden on my mind
a never ending pain in my heart.
A "wish I would have made the right decision"
kind of situation.
Perfection that never got its start.
A joy that was never held onto
a true happiness taken away
too fast.
A love that was sewn into my heart;
but still a love that didn't last.
Your memory is one
to which I have many feelings
but I still can't find the words to say
I wish it was one
I couldn't remember...
I wish I could write you away.

Love Poems

All I know are these love poems.
The kind that get you through
the night.
The ones that counsel you,
let you know you're not alone,
or everything will be alright.
All I know are these love poems.
The kind that release your pain
or help you tell a loved one
sunshine comes
after their rain.
All I know are these love poems
words worth more
than pearls and diamond rings
For there is nothing better than love
when it trusts, forgives, and bears
all things.

Reflection

Looking back on the past…
School, friends, relationships
all that didn't last.
The tears, the heartbreaks
the "love"
that wasn't love.
The reason change
was needed
and so often thought of.
Looking back on all
that wasn't
and could never be
Everyone who once
meant so much to me.
Everything I wanted
to hold on to
but my hands
couldn't grasp.
The good times
that I prayed would last.
Awesome times,
awesome friends,
even the funniest
of the funny jokes.
The poems that the tears
and the smiles wrote.
The song that constantly plays
in my heart,
the chosen selection.
I am thankful for the year
that inspired this reflection.

The Struggle

Month to month
week to week
check to check
How are you livin'?
Comfortable or
Lackin' respect
for yourself?
Are you hustlin' for a dollar
or selling yourself
for a dime?
Are you the problem
instead of the solution?
Are you the cause of the crime, the lie,
the need for the hustle?
How are you standing strong
in the struggle?

Naked Truth

I stood in front of him.
Naked.
But fully clothed.
I was wide open.
Heart
Mind
Soul
Everything.
Fears
Fantasies
Dreams
All of the answers
to his questions…
He could have it all.
No lies.
Complete truth.
I was ready
to be loved
for who I was
underneath
the protection.
That's the direction
I planned to go in.
Completely me.
Fully clothed,
yet completely naked,
and willing.

Dreamer

I'm a dreamer.
I sit and I contemplate this.
Weigh the pros and the cons
of whether I hit
or I miss.
I consider the what ifs
but I'm stuck
on the why nots.
I have to shoot for the moon
just to secure a spot.
I have to believe in my dreams
and to my heart I must stay true
Because if I believe in myself,
Someday
so will you.

Stronger

I used to wonder
why I was the one crying
why my boyfriend was the one lying
why I wouldn't stop trying
to please an unsatisfied man,
an unhappy man, a confused man.
I used to wonder
why I was constantly getting betrayed
and why there were teardrops
on the pillows
where my head laid.
I used to wonder
why I was on the outside looking in
how I'd get an enemy
from a friend
and why my broken heart
was one that couldn't mend.
I used to wonder how
I'd get sunshine from the rain
how joy would erase my pain
how when I was older
I would appreciate all that happened
when I was younger
until I learned
it was building my character
and making me stronger.

Good Enough

You've already shown me
you've got your mind made up
and although my best was my best
for you
even that wasn't good enough.
All the effort
in vain
only tears
to release my pain
things would never
and could never be the same.
Because you've already shown me
you had your mind made up
and although my best
was my best
for you
it just wasn't good enough.

Inspiration

I thought my inspiration died
when my broken heart healed.
My tears and confusion
caused my pen
to need a refill
and then it stopped.
One day I was inspired
and the next I was lost.
The tears helped me write
the love wouldn't let go
my reward all on paper
my life all for show.
My inspiration hadn't died
just a chapter complete
now time to get ready
for the new me.

LOST

(For my Aunt, Georgia Ann Logan.
May your presence always be
remembered and your truth honored.)

Lost inside a body
with someone else's mind
the original
somewhere stuck in time.
What do you do
when the medication
is all that will keep you sane?
What do you do when "schizophrenic"
is mentioned in the same breath
with your name?
When you're talking to yourself
and no one's even there?
When the rest of the world
is unaware
that you are
lost
inside of a body
with someone else's mind
Your original self…
Somewhere stuck in time?

Full

So used to you
attempting to tear me down
maybe one day
you'll choose to build me up.
And instead of trying to prove
how empty my glass is
maybe one day
you'll fill my cup.
Maybe you'll begin to motivate
and encourage
instead of planting seeds
of negativity in my mind
and maybe you'll see
a drastic change in me
if you're a little more supportive
over time.
So used to you
attempting to tear me down
maybe one day
you'll choose to build me up
and instead of trying to prove
how empty my glass is
maybe one day
You'll fill my cup.

My Ancestor's Child

I stand on the backs of many women
who fought and died.
I move beyond the shadows
of all who hurt and cried.
The women who marched
for a vote, a chance, a better day
women who knew
there was a better way.
I stand on the backs of many women
and I stand firm
because through their fight
and struggle
I was given a turn
to be more than average
more than the norm
to know a day would come
when I didn't have to conform.
When I didn't have to be
what a typical woman
was to be
a day when I was allowed to be me
allowed to succeed.
I stand on the backs of many women
their tears not in vain
Their screams, their cries,
their hurt, their pain
all during a time
when none of them could understand
they were paving the way
for me to have a chance.
They were planting the seeds
for the trees
that I'd need.
The hope, the courage,
the strength to believe…
in the smallest things.
I stand on the backs of many women
and I stand proud…
So Blessed
to be my Ancestor's Child.

Your Daughter

Give your daughter
the love she needs
so she doesn't search for it
in a man.
So she doesn't compromise
her morals
just to feel
a comforting hand.
Give your daughter
the love she needs
so she can focus
on her youth
so she won't be dressing
just to impress
people who don't respect
her truth.
Give your daughter
the love she needs
so she doesn't chase others
for validation.
Love her.
Listen to her
so people don't put her
in sticky situations.
Give your daughter
the love she needs
teach her to be humble
and not full of pride.
Protect her.
Teach her to respect her,
and all she possesses inside.

Love Us.

Sometimes we give love
too much of our space
too much of our being
and our time.
Too much of it
to others
those deserving and undeserving.
Sometimes we need to hold on to it
give it to ourselves.
Turn it inward
instead of outward
look into the mirror
instead of out the window
say "I love me"
instead of "I love you."
We need to love us.
First.

Perfectly Imperfect

I'd be lying
if I said I'm always okay.
I'm not.
And that's okay.
I've learned to accept
being perfectly imperfect.
In fact,
I pride myself on the imperfections
the things I can't change
can't fix
can't repair.
They are all okay
because it's completely okay
to be imperfect.

Love You

I grew up longing
for a love I couldn't find
Validation from everyone
who decided to give me time.
I needed them to remind me
of all God called me to be
I needed them to love me…
to support me
to encourage me
to believe in me.
I looked and looked
I gave a gave
I cried and cried.
Held my heart when it would
break inside.
I was always looking for love
but it was the type
no one else could give
it was the type I had to find
Within.
It was my love
I needed most.

My Feelings

I often find myself
in this space I hate…
a deep dark place.
Some would call it
my feelings.
I'd like to describe it
as a place of deep thought.
Love gained.
Love lost.
The place where
I've paid the cost
but I'm the boss.
My feelings.

Gave It All

I gave it all.
Every ounce.
Every thought.
Every piece I could share…
I gave it.
Every bit of everything
I could ever give away…
I gave it.
And every bit of me
was taken
until it was no longer wanted.
Everything was accepted
until it was no longer needed
until it was too real
to be reciprocated
too authentic to be duplicated
too strong to be appreciated…
I gave it all.

Goodness

We should never regret
giving the goodness away
even if we want to.
The goodness adds more light to the world
even if the outcome
hurts you.
The giving is necessary
in a world that lacks
peace
it brightens areas
so full of darkness
that average light
won't reach.
We have to keep giving.
Keep loving.
Keep living.
Keep hugging.
Keep shining our light.

Paper Boy

Big time
in the spotlight
picture with your face.
I remember holding you
in my arms
now I'm wishing
I was in your girl's place.
I sometimes don't understand
how you noticed me before
or what happened between us
that made you not notice me anymore.
But then there's your picture
with you all in the spotlight
now I'm wondering
is this what happened
is it because people say
you're so tight?
I wish I knew the reason
for this
or at least why my heart
got destroyed
I hope this paper didn't change you
or your feelings
Paper boy.

Leave You Behind

As the future becomes the present
now becomes the time
when I have to do what's right for me
when I have to leave you behind.
I never said good-bye to you
I just walked away
I didn't turn around to look
there's no way that I could stay.
Tears were overflowing inside
but not enough to pull me back
I knew you'd never know the truth
because it hid in the way I act.
I know you were perfect for me
but this is a chance I must take
and if I get to come back to you
I'll mend the heart
I didn't mean to break.
If we meet again
we were meant to be
and I'll surely make you mine
but I have to take that chance
I have to know…
so I gotta leave you behind.

Ghetto

Paint a perfect picture
of people dying to survive
doing anything to make money
to save their family's lives.
Drug dealers on every corner
violence in the air
people afraid to drive by
fearing they'll be shot
if they stop or stare.
Looks so uncomfortable
sun tinted instead of shining bright
danger so popular
people afraid to go out at night.
Carjackings, robberies, drive-bys,
gangsters, gang bangers, ex-cons
standing around looking for trouble
whether it's dusk or dawn.
But the negativity's only in mind
the ways this place is seen
is negative to those that are blind.
The one place where people are strong
enough to live
a life that most people wouldn't
consider to give.
The best place to find unity
True people who won't say no
Safe to some
but still dangerous
and only in the ghetto.

Master of My Heart

Just like all masters
you hold the key to what's yours
not even aware
that you still have the power
you had before.
It's all in your hands
you took they key from the start
and no one can steal your throne
you're the master of my heart.
Your actions can turn my happiness
into sadness or pain
but all I can do
is wish to have you
and hope someday you'll feel the same.
It's hard to believe you don't know
what high position you hold
it seems my heart belongs to you
even as memories grow old.
No other love can compare to yours
whether we're together or apart
and as long as it's up to me
you'll hold the key,
You're the master of my heart.

He'll Never Know

When I see him I get so speechless
that I can't speak
so I let him pass.
When he's next to me
I get so nervous
because my heart just beats so fast.
I can't build up the courage
to be comfortable around him
and my feelings I shall never show
I wish he felt this way for me…
because I love him
but he'll never know.
His slightest touch makes me quiver
his simplest words make me smile
and if love could go any distance
my love for him
would go on for miles.
It's hard to fight this feeling
and when I try they refuse to let go
I wish he felt this way for me…
Because I love him
but he'll never know.
I'm too scared to ask
what's really up
or to even say how I feel inside
the possibility of rejection
tells me stop
or give up because I already tried.
I've never had feelings so true
and it hurts to let them show
I wish he felt this way for me…
because I love him
but he'll never know.

All Over Again

I've been love's fool since the first time
I fell in love
I've given my all
to people who didn't give theirs
and in the end
I try to be strong
so I won't be hurt
by those who don't care.
I've given my heart to a perfect love
who won't give his heart to me
and I've been the one
to pick up the pieces
when no one could fulfill my needs.
I've been hurt by one too many
and I've been a best friend to heartache
I've given more than plenty
just to say "I've made a big mistake."
I've been a familiar friend to teardrops
like a sister to heartbreak and red eyes
I've been my sun when there was none
and only dark clouds in my skies.
I've been the only one seeing it all
first hand
I've been here
through thick and thin
and it's still hard to understand
how I pick up the pieces
and start all over again.

Wasted Years

I've wasted years of my life
on untrue love
I've wasted the best years of my life
for nothing.
I've wasted years of my life
on someone who now I never think of
I've wasted the best years of my life
for nothing.
I've wasted a year of my life
on a fairytale love
I've wasted a year of my life
to say this is the end
I've wasted one of the best years
of my life
I've wasted it to say
"We can't even be friends."
I've wasted years of my life
pushing myself
and making myself go for it
I've wasted tears
and what could have been the best years
of my life
and now
I have nothing to show for it.

Just Write

Sometimes
all I want to do is write.
Sometimes
writing is all that matters to me.
This ink
on this paper
is the only place
I find understanding.
The only place
even I understand me.
Feelings of anger, confusion,
pain…
joy, happiness, love, maintained.
Through this writing
is where I process
and assess.
Re-evaluate.
Re-calculate.
If any of it is actually worth it
or if it's all in my mind.

Uncut

Never imagined
this would be so painful
the opening up of me…
The self discovery.
I never imagined
all the things my eyes would see
when I removed the blindfold.
The things my heart would feel
with my truth told.
I never imagined
it would be painful.
Too many people
in my front row
not clapping
too many people in my boat
not rowing
They're waiting
for the show to end
or the boat to sink…
They clearly don't know me
and until recently…
neither did I.

Broken Decisions

Everyone I love
has hurt me.
Everyone.
Well almost.
The ones I let
get too close.
Family and friends…
Equally
contributing
to the damaging…
Willingly.
I'd like to say
it was an accident
but adults make choices…
actions
and voices
at their own will.
Now I have to heal…
from their decisions.

The Regret

If only I would have known,
I would've held on
just a little longer.
Stayed on the phone longer.
Muscled up the strength
to call you back.
Asked more questions.
Showed more care and concern.
And at the very least,
said "I love you."
If only
I would have known.
Such a valuable lesson learned.
One day the tears will be replaced
with smiles.
The regret,
with memories
and your love and memory
etched in stone.
I am a product
of one of your greatest deeds
and one of God's greatest Blessings
to both of us.
I hope you are looking down
and I really hope you are proud…
of me.

The Truth.

My heart needs it
yearns for it
and cries for it.
A time when the truth is
all that matters.
Was it her he desired?
Was it her he pursued?
Was it me too blind to see
what may have been the truth?
All the nights
I laid next to him
was it her he longed to have?
Was it her he wanted to know better
so she could make him laugh?
The first time
when the truth is all that matters,
it's the truth I can't find.
My heart wishing he only wanted me
but my thoughts saying I'm blind.
The pursuit that hurt
my feelings
more than my heart
the pursuit
that makes my world fall apart.
She could never compare
to me,
she couldn't be me
or do the things I do,
but she still has something
I don't;
She has the truth.

Hard to Forget

I'm in a place
I don't want to be
Mentally
Flashbacks of what he did to me
My heart
so torn apart
so long ago
but still I remember.
Not when it happened
exactly
but the feeling
the pain
the anger
and the shame.
The questions.
I thought he loved me.
Who's to blame?
The friendships
where too many words
were said
the heartache
still haunts my heart
and my head.
Once again
I'm in a place
I don't want to be
Mentally.
Having flashbacks
of what he did to me.
My heart
so torn apart
so long ago…
but still I remember.

Flowered Light

Flowers already bloomed
represent sunshine
in the room.
A bright light
in a dark place
a genuine smile
replacing an unhappy face.
Bloomed flowers
represent life
hugs and kisses
on cold nights
love and joy
of life…
consumed
all in the flowers
already bloomed.

The Way

The violence.
The guns.
The lives
Lost.
The tears.
The pain.
The total
Cost.
Someone who expected
to breathe
Life
tonight
died
Today.
Someone
looking forward
to getting back
home
was
Murdered
on the way
because someone
Lost
their way.

Waiting Forever

I'm dreading tomorrow.
I knew good-bye would come
Someday
but not someday soon.
Never had to miss one person
Forever.
They say the pain will ease up
Eventually.
I can't even think straight.
Waiting for the day
when it doesn't hurt so much.
Waiting for the day
when they tell me what happened
and explain why
you're no longer here.
I'm waiting for justice
or understanding.
For peace and comfort.
For the feeling or confirmation
that you're okay…
wherever you are.
I'm waiting for someone
to wake me up from this nightmare
waiting for your call
waiting for your message
waiting…
Forever.

The Memories I Choose

I remember the white tennis shoes
the snap back hats
the days you bought donuts
by the dozen
the black and white bike for Christmas
the ridiculously loud music
your silver Audi
and the purple mustang you tried
to get me to buy from your neighbor.
I remember the disappointment
the plans we almost had
and the times I wished you were there
but I couldn't find you.
I remember so many things
but what I remember most
is our last call.
I remember you asking
how I was doing
how everyone else was doing
how my job was going
I remember you saying you were glad
that I was happy.
I remember your "This is B. Wake" messages
but most of all
I remember your smile
and how your face would light up
when I would pop up
Unexpectedly.
I will always remember you loved me.
I will always remember you.

Triangle

Some chick cried
when my friend got pregnant.
Not even in secrecy either.
Her dude acted like
he didn't see her...
I did though.
Suspect...
If you know what I know.
But my friend,
She cried over someone else
when he got engaged...
Some high school Boo
but she couldn't eat for days.
He was that dude
that made her feel
whole in so many ways.
And who was I to tell her
to move on?
I was no expert at
letting go of love
when it seems gone.
I just offered comfort.
Told her I was here.
Provided her some tissue
for those uncontrollable tears.
Couldn't figure out why they were together...
Neither of them wanted to be here...
Clearly.

Anxious

Heart racing
Eyes opened
Am I dying
Or is life joking?
This was it.
The more I worried
The faster the pace
My mind...
All over the place.
He died in his sleep
So I couldn't sleep
Thinking of all the plans
He'd never see.
My fear
Took over me.
Heart racing
Eyes open
Arms jumping
Heart broken
Is life playing?
Am I dying?
Am I staying?
Emergency room
Please save me...
I'm only 31...
Technically still a baby.
I can't breathe
They said to wait
Lobby seat
My mom prayed...
Told me I would be okay.
They said it was stress
Causing anxiety those days.
The pain of losing my father
Brought so much fear to my mind
That and when I had that accident
That time.
Crushed between two cars
Driver not paying attention
Less than one year prior
I should mention.
Only 30...
Body looked fine
Most of the trauma
Embedded in my mind.
My neck, my back,
My shoulders...
That fear.
And all within two short years.
Heart racing...
Eyes opened.
Am I dying?
Or is life joking?
They said it was just anxiety.

The Observation

That walk though…
Y'all know who he is.
Hella sexy
has hella kids…
I'm just assuming.
My assumptions aren't facts.
I'm just saying…
I'm sure more than one
has tried
to put a lock on that.
Tried to find ways
to hold on for life.
Having his babies
if they can't be his wife…
That type.
None of it works though
because his heart
is blocked and protected
Held by the only female
he actually respected.
And she knows it.
Because he told her.
Not when they were young
but when they got much older
and she feels exactly the same…
Sometimes
feelings never change.

Hide and Seek

Sometimes we hide in obvious places
where no one can see us.
See our flesh…yes
but the real us
is invisible.
We hurt where no one knows
where surface relationships
never go
where small talk
will never know.
Right there.
That's the place we hide.
The place where you cry
in the car
and get out with a smile
the place where you feel
completely alone
in the middle of a crowd…
That place.
Where only God and time
can heal or reach
where the speakers have no speech
and the arms have no reach.
That place.
Down deep.

You Don't Know Me

If you don't meet me in this space
where my soul resides
where I completely let go
of my pride
and reveal all that I usually hide,
you don't really know me.
I'm sure of it.
If you never see my face
when I speak of my dreams…
If I've never discussed my dreams
with you…
you don't know me.
Not the real version.
You know the protection.
The mask.
The coating.
The Do. Not. Pass. Go.
without permission
Version
of who I am.
But you don't know me.
Because underneath
all of that
I'm vulnerable
and beautiful
and open…
Even when I'm broken.
So if you never meet me there…
In that space
where we are both honest, and hopeful,
and open
and unashamed of our broken…
you don't know me
and you never will.
I'm sure of it.

For A While

I haven't been myself for a while now
forgotten how it feels to love
forgotten what it feels like to be free
I've buried my true feelings
to be a part of what's in my heart
maybe looking for another start.
But I've neglected what means most
I've let my life slip down the drain.
Damn, I feel like I'm going insane.
I can't help but to wonder
how things would've been,
could've been,
should've been.
Now look at all this mess I'm in.
But I miss me.
I miss the caring,
the sharing, the love, and the smiles.
I haven't been myself
for a while now.

Love Like You
(for poetry)

I've never had a love like you
even though you weren't my first
You're always there, in my thoughts
Comforting, when I'm hurt.
I've never had a love like you
love that never turns its back
a love that remains just the same
whether I gain or I lack.
I've never had a love like you
that allows me to be myself
to express myself openly
without negative opinions
from anyone else.
I've never had a love like you
and although you share it,
You're one of a kind
and I love you more than anything
Whether I'm doing bad or I'm fine.
I've never had a love like you.

Never Understand

The way I feel
no one could feel
the way I hurt
no one could hurt.
The way I cry
no one could cry.
The pain I feel
is enough for a family
enough pain for a state
enough pain for not enough people
not enough people to relate.
The way I hurt
is enough hurt to last for years
maybe a decade.
Too much hurt for one person
too much hurt to accept in one day.
The way I cry…
I shed enough tears to create a lake
or maybe a sea
I shed enough tears
for my tears to drown me.
Feeling all this emotion
because things didn't go as I planned
feeling all this emotion
that I will never understand.

Good Woman

I bet you don't even know
you have a good woman.
You're too blind to have
realized such a thing.
You're too worried about what other
women have to offer
to realize what a good woman can bring.
A good woman brings you understanding
she listens when no one else will
and when you doubt her value
in your life
she makes it clear, just like her love,
She's for real.
A good woman holds your hand
when you don't want to walk alone
she accepts your strengths
as well as your weaknesses
she realizes when you've grown.
A good woman does not "do as you say"
she does what she knows is right.
She stands up for her own beliefs
even if she has to sleep alone at night.
A good woman does not walk behind you
she walks right by your side
she makes it evident that she loves you
but God is the only man she needs in her life.
A good woman will be your lover,
your best friend, your ear, your shoulder,
and for you she will do all that she can.
A good woman will bring to your life positive things
she might even make you a good man.

Invisible Scars

They wonder why we act the way we act
and why we do what we do
but while they're paying so much attention
to our outside
our insides hold the truth.
From broken dreams to broken hearts
we bury ourselves in sorrow
running from the past
but too afraid to lean towards tomorrow.
With low self-esteem and put downs
we can't help but to ask why
holding our heads down
instead of holding them high.
Friends lost and loved ones gone
we wonder what the future brings
we wonder how we can be strong
with what we've been through
and all we've seen.
Still they wonder why we act the way we act
why we seem so negative
but how can we be so generous
when so many people take
instead of letting us give?
With all of the tears and times of pain
it seems we won't get far
unless we take time to try
to heal our wounds
and get rid of our invisible scars.

Real Love

Never ending
never doubting
wait for you forever
type of love.
Real love doesn't fade.
It's the kind of love
when you can still
taste your first kiss
or feel the first time you smiled
or your first hug.
It's that kind of love
when you remember
the first time you spoke
on the phone
or even felt lonely alone.
Real love is the kind where
the good times fail to fade
even when the bad ones
are constantly replaying
in your head.
Real love is that love
that will make you risk it all
just for one more chance.
Even an uncertain one.
It's the kind that'll cause you
to still hold on
even though in the world's eyes
the love is gone.
Real love doesn't allow you to forget.
Won't allow you to regret.
Can't allow you to shake
the memory
of when you first met.
It's that love that
you feel deep in your heart
and down in your soul
even when your mind tells you
to let go
That's when you'll know…
You've found real love.

Gold Digger

Hey, What's your name again?
Hmmm. You're lookin' fine!
Your Versace shirt looks nice
and I love the way your platinum shines.
Your diamonds are just gleaming.
Your suit is one of a kind.
How can I get to know you?
What do you say?
Your place or mine?
Your left pocket is looking large.
How many bills are inside?
I've never seen a car like that before
let's go on a ride.
Would you let me drive it
if I told you I'd be cool?
I promise I'll drive slow
I won't act a fool.
But how can I get to know you
so I can share the finer things?
The cars, the clothes, the money,
and especially those platinum rings?!
Do I have dirt under my fingernails?
Or a shovel in my pocket?
I should have had green eyes?!
What?! Boy, you need to stop it!
I do this all the time?!
What do you mean?
How do you figure?
I just want the finer things in life…
I am NOT a Gold Digger!

Our Condolences

On days when the sun has yet to shine
or rain begins to fall
there's always someone praying
for strength
or someone who's lost it all.
There are those whose lives are full of joy
and others live with sorrow and pain
but after the darkest day ends
the sun will shine again.
No one could know
exactly how you feel
even if they ask
for only you know what's real
because you have memories that will last.
Just remember you are not alone
regardless of how you feel
the Lord is watching you from home
and your wounds He'll surely heal.
And regardless of the troubles
each day may bring
one thing is surely true,
Praying will get you through anything.
Our condolences go out to you.

Now I'll Rest

I looked down and saw you crying
I wondered the reason why
we never knew I'd be dying
so I didn't say good-bye.
He called while I was sleeping
he said it was my time
And I shall never look back and worry
he told me you'll be fine.
Every task that I started
was meant for me to do
and if I left any incomplete
if possible, they'll be completed by you.
He said no matter how much it hurt
you'll find the strength and be strong
and even though it sounds impossible
one day you'll move on.
He put me in your life for that day,
season, month, or year
and even though I'm gone,
please celebrate
no need to shed those tears.
For I did all I was put here to do
and God knows I did my best
just make sure to take care of you
for it's my time to rest.

Before

Before you left me, you loved me.
Before you loved me, you liked me.
Before you liked me, you cared.
And before you cared,
you made sure
I was aware.
Before I was aware
you made effort
before you made effort, you made a choice
you made a choice whether you'd use
your actions or your voice.
Before you made that choice
you wondered if it should begin
and before then,
we were just friends.
But not anymore.

Follow Your Heart

The only way to find happiness
is to listen to your soul
the main controller which is your heart
will lead you to your destined road.
Where dreams become reality
and true love is first felt
you must follow your heart
even if the toes you step on
belong to someone else.
The things you'll find by listening
won't be found any other time
and the feeling you might think is love
won't be true in your heart, just your mind.
So you make the choice to be happy,
Choose right or choose wrong.
If the road your heart will lead to
makes you sad,
it won't be for long.
If you want to erase or prevent the tears
just listen for the call
Just keep an open mind
to whatever happens
and in the end you'll stand tall.
You have to think for yourself
because your decision is the most important part.
Just remember if you want to be happy
you have to follow your heart.

For Your Protection

I've been there and done that
so now I sit back and observe
I notice how they come at you
with those same old tired words.
So I make a choice, I watch,
or I take out the shield
to protect you from receiving wounds
that only time can heal.
And while trying to keep you happy
I dig up the past
the hurt, the pain,
questions unanswered but asked.
I shield you from the heartbreaks,
let downs, and lies
I protect you so there's happiness
instead of pain in your eyes.
For I've hurt enough for both of us
and I've cried for two or three
so there's only room for one emotion
if you leave things up to me.
I'd go through it again to save someone
the hurt, lies, pain, heartbreak, and rejection
I'd do it to save the future
and definitely for your protection.

He's Good

He knows just what to do
and what to say
to get my forgiveness
when he has done things the wrong way.
The I love yous
and I miss yous
all sound good
but somewhere something
is misunderstood.
Yeah, he's good.
He knows just when
to erase the pages
or mess up the redial
on the phone
he knows the right spot
to keep the numbers
for the girls
when he's alone.
He knows just when to lie
or how to get out of it
when he's caught
he knows that if he gives in
things will forever be lost.
He's good.
He knows just when
to invite them over
and just when to make them leave
and he's good at making his lies
something easy
to believe.
Yes, he's good.
Too bad I'm not stupid.

Denial

I wonder if I'm in denial.
Am I believing he can do
something he can't?
Am I expecting him to be
more than "a man?"
Am I believing his word
actually stands for
what it should?
Am I believing he actually could?
Be faithful, and caring,
and honest, and real?
Or am I in denial
about the whole ordeal?

Just To Know

Happiness, smiles, and joy
pain, tears, and lies
Love that comes and goes
in my heart and through my eyes.
Better to love
than to not have loved at all.
Better to have stumbled hard
than to not even have begun to fall.
Nothing like experiencing love
whether it's coming or going away
and there's nothing like receiving love
regardless of whether it can or can't stay.
For a true smile is smiled
when it's smiling from the heart
and real tears are cried
when true love falls apart.
Still tomorrow there's no promise
even if one was made
love is a wonderful experience
that only heart and mind can save.
In love you have no choices
for only fate can choose
but it's better just to know how love feels
whether you win or you lose.

Love Forever

Written in pen
on my letter before my name
I tell you how I'll feel
even if your feelings change.
My words are sincere
that's why they're in ink
I want you to understand
just how much you mean to me.
No doubts in your mind
should keep your feelings away
this evidence on paper
saying I love you, will always stay.
Now I could sign this with "Sincerely"
or "Yours Truly" even if we won't
always be together
But instead I'll make the thought last
and sign this with "Love Forever."

Sister 2 Sister

Can you tell me when we became separate?
When our attitudes changed?
Sometimes you don't even speak
and I know you know my name.
And even if you don't know it,
would it hurt to offer a smile?
Or a "Hey my sister, how are you doing?"
Instead of you looking off into the crowd.
Where did we get the pre-judgement from?
Where did we learn the rolling of the eyes?
When did we stop speaking to each other
and start spreading rumors and lies?
When did we become too good to speak
or acknowledge another queen?
Who said that without your sisters
you could fulfill all of your dreams?
"Together we stand, divided we fall"
is a statement that is definitely true
If it turns out that I have no one left
to lean on
my sister, I hope I could lean on you.
We needed each other in the past
I'm positive we'll need each other again
and even if we don't accept the fact
that we are sisters,
the least we could do
is be friends.

Written in Tears

I've shown my work to many people
I've let them in my world
I allowed them to enter
a restricted place
in the life of
this mature little girl.
They enjoy reading about my happiness
they agree when I speak
of truth and change
they love to learn of my progress
but get silent
when they read of my pain.
Of course some words
are from my imagination
but most come from my heart
words of love, words of joy
pure from their start.
I've been writing my life story
in poetry for years
some words written with hope and joy
but many,
written in tears.

Nothing Heals

Nothing heals a broken heart.
Not time.
Not space.
Not another love.
Nothing fills the hole
when that love was true.
Nothing.
Fixes you.
Last time
I buried mine.
6 feet deep…
helped me sleep.
Let me move on.
Just had to pretend
the love was gone.
Pretended he didn't exist
never spoke his name
never told anyone about him
just prayed my feelings would change…
or dissolve
or disappear
or I'd lose the memory
of ever having him here.
But none of it worked.
Because nothing can heal
my broken heart.
Except his love.

Magnitude

I made myself vulnerable
got my heart busted apart
pulled something from the grave…
resurrected something
that survived in the dark.
I freed it
happily
thinking it could handle the light
but it flourished beyond my control
couldn't even sleep well at night.
I mean this thing survived
the dark
beneath the surface…
the grave
it lived and maintained its strength
for decades more than days.
It survived without nourishment
attention or light.
It waited… patiently
until the time was right.
But once I set it free,
it was out of control
searching for the one
whose half makes me whole.
This thing…
This power…
This uncontrollable feeling people speak of…
Hearts. Stars. Fireworks… LOVE.

Out of Hope

I'm learning
that love isn't enough.
Feel like I've said this over and over
Again
And still
I'm tasked with learning
the same lesson.
We can love each other
Forever
And it will still never
be enough
If the effort
doesn't match up.
Sometimes
the words don't even matter.
Eyes watering
Heart shattered…
Because love was supposed to be
Enough.

War

He said he'd go to war for it
with a serious face.
Said this was his space
and no one would take his place.
He was willing to fight for it
armored up or bare
He really didn't care.
He wanted to be there…
Here.
And he said it with a serious face.
Unfortunately
he never made it to war.
Barely made it to 4…
months.
No need to allow a war
when you've already decided
nothing is worth fighting for.

The Strongest

The strongest one is not
the most silent
Not the one who hides it
and not the one
who's the loudest either.
The strongest is neither
of those things.
It's the most vulnerable.
The one who's not afraid
to show their heart
and soul
The one who will love you
and fight to not have to let you go.
Even when the odds
are against them.
The strongest one
is not afraid to say
how they feel
even when pain
makes it all too real.
They'd prefer to be honest
and free
even if it's not what the world wants
them to be.
The strength comes
from not hiding or pretending
but from being authentic
from the beginning.
It is in our vulnerability
that we are strong.

Empty.

I said goodbye.
This time
I have to let go.
It hurts so much
in my heart and soul.
But I know
I can't hold on any longer.
My hands are bloodied
and I need to get stronger
for the other things
life has planned for me.
I wanted him
but he doesn't understand me.
I wanted us
but it doesn't matter anymore.
I gave so much
and I never kept score.
Now I'm empty.
Goodbye was all I had left.

ABOUT THE AUTHOR

Born and raised in Oakland, California, April Wakefield-Spikener began writing poetry as a young child as a way to express herself. She dreamed of someday becoming a famous poet... A day when people would fall in love with her way of thinking and writing. A self-proclaimed "Lover of Love," she writes from the heart, often capturing feelings most people don't discuss openly.

Sometimes people dream dreams and other times they live them.

Thank you for taking time to experience mine.

April S

Stay Connected:

Instagram: @aprilthepoet
Facebook: April Wakefield-Spikener Poetry
Email: AprilThePoet@aprilolivia.com

www.ingramcontent.com/pod-product-compliance
Lightning Source LLC
Chambersburg PA
CBHW071413090426
42737CB00011B/1452
* 9 7 8 0 6 9 2 9 1 6 9 1 9 *